SPOOKY SUDBURY

SPOOKY SUDBURY

True Tales of the Eerie & Unexplained

Mark Leslie & Jenny Jelen

DUNDURN
TORONTO

Copyright © Mark Leslie Lefevre and Jenny Jelen, 2013

All rights reserved. No part of this publication may be reproduced, stored in a retrieval system, or transmitted in any form or by any means, electronic, mechanical, photocopying, recording, or otherwise (except for brief passages for purposes of review) without the prior permission of Dundurn Press. Permission to photocopy should be requested from Access Copyright.

Editor: Laura Harris
Design: Jennifer Scott
Printer: Webcom

Library and Archives Canada Cataloguing in Publication

Leslie, Mark, 1969-, author
Spooky Sudbury : true tales of the eerie & unexplained / Mark Leslie and Jenny Jelen.

Includes bibliographical references.
Issued in print and electronic formats.
ISBN 978-1-4597-1923-1 (pbk.).--ISBN 978-1-4597-1924-8 (pdf).--ISBN 978-1-4597-1925-5 (epub)

1. Ghosts--Ontario--Sudbury. 2. Haunted places--Ontario--Sudbury. I. Jelen, Jenny, author II. Title.

BF1472.C3L475 2013   133.109713'133   C2013-903913-9   C2013-903914-7

1 2 3 4 5   17 16 15 14 13

We acknowledge the support of the **Canada Council for the Arts** and the **Ontario Arts Council** for our publishing program. We also acknowledge the financial support of the **Government of Canada** through the **Canada Book Fund** and **Livres Canada Books**, and the **Government of Ontario** through the **Ontario Book Publishing Tax Credit** and the **Ontario Media Development Corporation**.

Care has been taken to trace the ownership of copyright material used in this book. The author and the publisher welcome any information enabling them to rectify any references or credits in subsequent editions.

J. Kirk Howard, President

Printed and bound in Canada.

The publisher is not responsible for websites or their content unless they are owned by the publisher.

Visit us at
Dundurn.com | @dundurnpress | Facebook.com/dundurnpress | Pinterest.com/dundurnpress

Dundurn	Gazelle Book Services Limited	Dundurn
3 Church Street, Suite 500	White Cross Mills	2250 Military Road
Toronto, Ontario, Canada	High Town, Lancaster, England	Tonawanda, NY
M5E 1M2	LA1 4XS	U.S.A. 14150

For those who decided to stay.
And for those, no longer with us,
who stay in our hearts.

"Sudbury can be viewed as a 'constellation city' made up of individual, smaller communities, each with its own attributes, forming a whole that is greater than the sum of its parts."

— Oiva W. Saarinen,
*From Meteorite Impact to Constellation City:
A Historical Geography of Greater Sudbury*

TABLE OF CONTENTS

Note on the Stories	13
Foreword by Mitch Ross	15
Preface: There's No Curbing This Sudbury Spirit by Jenny Jelen	19
Acknowledgements	23
Introduction: Monsters in My Closet and in My Head — Why Sudbury Has Always Been Spooky to Me	25

SUDBURY SPOOKS: GHOSTS, SPECTRES, AND OTHER APPARITIONS
45

We Can't Be the Only Things Here	47
A Ghost He Couldn't Leave Behind	50
Haunted 2650 Level of Levack Mine	53
Sydney Brown's Undying Passion for the Theatre	59
Wanapitei's North River Graveyard	63
Stay Away From Joe Lone's Place	67
Charlie Smith's Ghost	72
Runoff	78
The Man She Never Met	80
Reassuring Encounters	82
Cindy's Guardian Angel	85
The Bell Mansion	87

I'll Be Back 96

Along the North Shore 99

Capreol Red and the Capreol High Custodian 101

The Entity in Halloween House 104

The Energies Present 108

The Hospital 112

Morgan Road 115

The Chelmsford Ghost 118

The Nickel Miner's Ghost 122

SCARY SUDBURY SKIES: 127
UFOs, FLYING SAUCERS, AND OTHER OBJECTS IN THE SKY

We Are Not Alone 129

The 1950s: The Race to (and from) Space 133

The 1960s: Did You Detect That Movement in the Sky? 146

The 1970s: The Scramble Over Falconbridge 153

The 1980s and Beyond: Wherefore Art Thou? 160

Do You Hear What I See? 164

The Hunter and the Hunted 167

SPECULATIVE SUDBURY: 175
BIGFOOT, SASQUATCH, AND OTHER STRANGE CREATURES

Big Sightings of Large-Footed Cryptid Creatures 177

The Creature from Big Trout Lake 181

STRANGE SUDBURY: 185
OTHER ODDITIES, EERIE ENCOUNTERS, AND STRANGENESS

Blood and Darkness	187
The Weird Kid: Rob Sacchetto	190
Which Witch Do You Imagine When Someone Says "Witch"?	192
The Defiant Empire of Brigitte Kingsley	195
The Enigma of Tom Morley	197
Sudbury Region Ghost Towns	201
Underground Ghost Hunters and the Search for Dark Matter	207
Northern Ontario's Lord of Gore: Peter Mihaichuk	211
The Donnellys' Tombstone	214
The Old Hag Held Me Down While Aliens Abducted My God Helmet!	217

SPOOKY RESOURCES: 225
USEFUL AND INTERESTING RESOURCES FOR FURTHER READING AND EXPLORATION OF THE SUDBURY REGION

Places	228
Websites and Other Online Resources	233
Publications and Books	241
Notes	255

NOTE ON THE STORIES

From the humble beginnings to the booming mining years, Sudbury has played host to stories of wealth and prosperity, hardship and struggle, and everything in between. Through the highs and the lows come tales of great success and great despair, adding to the wonder of a city that, by land area, is the largest city in Ontario.

Sudbury is home to the Big Nickel, a thirty foot replica of a 1951 Canadian Nickel and the Inco Superstack, which, until 1987, was the world's largest free-standing chimney at 1250 feet. Science North, Northern Ontario's most popular interactive science museum is in Sudbury, and the city also boasts a vibrant arts community. With over 330 lakes within the city limits, it is an outdoor lover's wonderland, rich with various seasonal sports, and the birthplace of more than eighty NHL hockey players.

But there are other strange things afoot in this peaceful northern municipality; things not readily visible, but which lurk just beneath the surface.

And despite the vow so many people have of "trying to leave" this northern community for other destinations, something about

SPOOKY SUDBURY

the Nickel City keeps luring them back. Whether it's the taste of fresh air — or just the sulphur in the air — it's hard to move beyond the black rocks, endless lakes and great openness without longing to come home.

From a ghost seen wandering level 2650 of a local mine to voices and strange sounds heard in the basement of an abandoned hospital; from a graveyard that seems to protect itself from unwelcome visitors to a series of inexplicable lights regularly reported hovering in the night sky; from reports of strange creatures stalking the northern woods to eerie encounters, restless spirits and other unexplainable phenomenon that go bump in the night.

Spooky Sudbury explores the magnetic aura surrounding the city, for the living as well as the once-alive, in tales of mystery, wonder, and outright horror.

FOREWORD

When I was asked to write the foreword of this book, I naturally asked "Why me?" My natural neurosis immediately kicked in. What made me the Creepy Guy? Was it my cologne, or maybe my sense of dress? I thought my trench coat was stylish!

With a laugh, the authors reassured me that they were looking for someone with local knowledge of creepy things.

That I do have.

The city of Greater Sudbury has a long and very interesting history. It would be nearly impossible to grow up here and not have heard a strange and unexplained story of one kind or another.

In the 1950s Sudbury was a hotbed of UFO activity. In 1975, four UFOs were confirmed on radar, and fighter jets were sent to the area from an air force base in Michigan.

Perhaps it was a result of the cold war, an increase in visibility through movies and television shows that made our city more active for these types of occurrences. Or, maybe it's something else.

Spooky Sudbury

Greater Sudbury is a mid-sized Canadian city (pop. 160,000) with an industrial resource base; a bustling community that is the centre of commerce for northeastern Ontario. Nestled in the Canadian Shield, it is surrounded by a natural, rugged beauty that reflects the friendly and self-reliant nature of its inhabitants. It is everything you'd expect from a city of its size — big city amenities with a small-town feel. At least that's what you'd think.

There's something more here, though. As one might find with the American Deep South, underneath this placid, genial exterior lurks something almost … sinister.

As with any city, there are sudden deaths. Some are violent, others unexpected, and all are tragic. The sense of small-town closeness can begin to feel suffocating as tales of jealous lovers, disappearances, murder, suicide, and accidental death increase

The Sudbury Region houses unique blends of rugged natural beauty with an underlying energy as deep and dark as the mines the city was built upon.

FOREWORD

in size as people engage in the child's game of "telephone" and the story is embellished as it passes from ear to ear.

Unfortunately, locals have had more than their share to gossip about. Some years Sudbury has had almost one murder per month, sometimes more — a statistic well above the rate of other cities of comparable size.

The community has also had several high-profile, unsolved homicides, some of which have garnered national attention. And, there have been many strange disappearances.

Some of these people are not the type to run away or to get lost. Stories range from women who've vanished from seemingly happy domestic lives, to experienced men who never returned from hunting and fishing trips.

Of course, it's likely that many of these stories have elements of the aforementioned party game syndrome and that most have some rational explanation.

But, as a final thought, consider this:

I've been told by local First Nations elders that the core of what is now the city of Greater Sudbury was traditionally considered to be a place best avoided. In fact, the whole area was believed to have a strong energy to it, but that the center in particular was a dark place.

I was told that this is the reason that no First Nations settlement was ever established at the heart of our city, and that communities were instead erected at its borders. Such was the fear of that dark energy.

These elders told me that there are stories of people who disappeared when traversing the land, and tales of others who went mad after travelling across the area. There are also stories of sudden and uncharacteristic violent acts by people that are attributed to this piece of land.

Strangely, many of these stories mirror modern occurrences

SPOOKY SUDBURY

with only minor cultural and historical differences. It would seem there is still an energy that runs as dark and deep as the mines the city is built upon.

So, is that *creepy* enough for you?

Enjoy the book.

Mitch Ross
President ORP.ca
Overlord of ParaNorthern.ca
Spring 2013

PREFACE: THERE'S NO CURBING THIS SUDBURY SPIRIT

I have a tendency to be a little bit impulsive, and sometimes I struggle to contain my enthusiasm. I occasionally say things before I think them through, and I often get tangled up in the moment. Keep that in mind as you read on.

It was just another day at the office when I first "met" Mark Leslie. During business hours, I am the entertainment and lifestyle reporter for *Northern Life*, Sudbury's community newspaper. Mark and I had an interview lined up to talk about his book *Haunted Hamilton*. I've always loved reading about ghosts and paranormal stuff, so naturally I was excited about the phone conversation we had scheduled.

During the interview, we talked about his childhood fear of monsters in the closet, and we talked about his career as a professional writer. We talked about growing up in Onaping Falls, and we talked about the family names we both knew. It was my job to ask the right questions to make the former Sudburian's book relevant to the local folks reading the paper. It only seemed fitting that I ask if he had plans to write a similar

SPOOKY SUDBURY

book about his hometown. According to my recollection, the conversation went something like this:

> Jenny: Have you ever thought about writing a collection of short ghost stories about Sudbury?
> Mark: Huh. (*Pauses to think about answer*)
> Jenny: Well, I think it's a great idea! If you want to do it, I'll even help!
> Mark: Ok.
> Jenny: Cool!

I'm not entirely sure how serious either of us was about the idea initially. But we must have both thought there was some value to it, as did Mark's connections at Dundurn Publishing, because, well, you are reading the result of that conversation.

Looks like that damn inability to keep my mouth shut has, in fact, worked out for the better. During the last few months, I've gotten an entirely different perspective of the city I know, love, and call home.

I already knew there were some amazing people living here and making the city a better place. What I didn't know was just how many non-living beings had stuck around.

The stories people have shared are nothing short of spectacular. After learning about Sydney Brown, I made a point of whispering "hi Syd" every time I walk into the Sudbury Theatre Centre. I no longer shrug off the vibes I get whenever I drive by the old hospital on Paris Street. And I certainly had a few sleepless nights along the way as well.

It's probably fair for me to tell you that I have never personally come in contact with a ghost. I've been in situations that left my skin sharp with goosebumps, but none of these experiences have ever made me think, "I just experienced something

Preface

During the writing of this book, author Jenny Jelen has gained an entirely different perspective of the city she loves.

paranormal." Despite my scatterbrained nature, I like to think I'm at least a little bit logical.

"There has to be a reason the cat keeps fixing his stare toward the living room, meowing that awful screechy meow. He probably just sees something outside. Maybe he's just bored."

Maybe there is more to it, but for the sake of sleeping comfortably at night, I choose not to explore it.

That being said, I'm open-minded about this sort of stuff. Just because we can't see or feel these things doesn't mean they don't exist, right? If you disagree, consider the same questions while contemplating the existence of your brain.

After compiling stories for this project, I think I would like to one day meet a ghost.

Who knows, maybe I'll even become one!

Jenny Jelen
Sudbury, Ontario 2013

Acknowledgements

The authors would like to thank all of the amazing people who took time to share stories, talk with us, write to us and otherwise relate tales that could be turned into elements that became a part of this book. Speaking, writing and connecting with you was an absolute pleasure and we can't thank you enough for being so willing to share your experiences, expertise and enthusiasm. In particular, we would like to thank Matthew Del Pappa, Kimberly Fahner, Michael Kavluk, Melanie Marttila, Charlie Smith, and Steve Vernon for letting us reproduce their eloquent words as part of their chapters. Thanks to Creepy Guy Mitch Ross for a helping hand to beautifully set the scene for the book's foreword. And thanks to Roger Czerneda, Steve Ripley, John Robbie, Greg Roberts, Eugene Lefebvre, and Rob Sacchetto for their amazing photos and images. The authors would also like to thank the great team at Dundurn, in particular Laura Harris, our editor, for her patience, vision, and guidance; Sheila Douglas, for keeping our paperwork in order and the project on track; for Beth Bruder and Margaret Bryant and the sales, marketing, and editorial team for believing in this project and the little northern Ontario city that could.

SPOOKY SUDBURY

JENNY'S NOTES

Confession: I had no idea how consuming a book writing project could be. It's a pretty big ordeal.

That being said, I'm so grateful for everyone who encouraged me to write, and especially to those who encouraged me to write well. Mick Lowe, thanks for the regular emails about style and flow (sorry about the short, choppy sentence I expressed this thanks in). Also, I don't think I'd have even tackled a project like this if it wasn't for your friendly spurring to continue pushing myself as a word person. I am so blessed to have the best of the best — people like you — to call my mentors.

Whitman the cat — I am not the least bit thankful for the eerie way you stared off into space, looking at something I apparently couldn't see, while I was compiling notes for the really scary stories. That's why I never made you fish sticks.

MARK'S NOTES

I would like thank two very important people for believing in and helping me, particularly the limitless patience that my beautiful wife Francine and my incredible son Alexander displayed while I spent countless evenings and weekends locked in the basement working madly on this book. My sequestered moments of writing and research are always met with support, good humour and enthusiasm that I appreciate more than I can ever express.

Introduction: Monsters in My Closet and in My Head — Why Sudbury Has Always Been Spooky to Me

As I revealed in the introduction to *Haunted Hamilton*, I am afraid of the monster under my bed. I'm also, of course, afraid of the monster in my closet, not to mention the one that is hiding under the stairs, just waiting to reach out from between the risers to grab my feet if I don't launch myself at full speed up the basement steps.

One of the reasons why I believe that I write the things I do is because, despite the fact that I've reached adulthood, in many ways I'm still the young child peeking out from under the covers at night in that small, remote mid-northern Ontario mining town; curious about what that strange sound was I had just heard and wondering if tonight could be the night that the creature under my bed will finally spring his trap and get me.

Thank goodness for the magically protective presence of bedcovers — so long as I keep my legs and feet, my hands and arms and my head covered, I'll be okay; the monster won't be able to get me. Yes, even in the dead heat of summer I need those covers or else that terrible creature might get me while I am at my most vulnerable.

SPOOKY SUDBURY

Please don't laugh. I know some of the people reading this feel the same way — although how many of you are willing to admit it?

And before you try to explain it to me, don't worry; I get it. I can sometimes be a bit irrational when it comes to the ghosties and goblins. When the morning sunlight slowly inches its way into my bedroom, dispelling the shadows and revealing that the space under my bed is 100 percent monster-free, abolishing any physical evidence of the monster I thought was there, I'm still not completely convinced.

That's because no amount of sunshine or logical reasoning could ever completely remove that monster from my mind.

Why is that?

I would argue it is because, despite the fact I never saw that monster, I still *knew* he was there. And since I never laid eyes on him, the image that I formed in my mind was far more powerful than anything I could have actually beheld.

Our imaginations do that to us. Good writers know this and draw upon that to make the stories they write even more horrifying — something that leaves an even bigger impression on our psyches. After all, our minds are far more powerful because they have access to our secret terrors and biggest fears. No matter how great a literary work can be, at best, those words help us to draw upon those things inside us that conjure up monsters far more terrifying than the things we actually see, hear, or read.

Writing about the paranormal works the same way. An author researches and then relays stories about frightening, disturbing, and eerie things; often situations and events that aren't easily explained.

Because subtle gaps are left to be filled, the reader's mind inserts its own hidden fears, insecurities, and terrors — the proverbial monsters under their own beds — making those words far more effective.

Introduction

Mark Leslie, captured in this 1979 encounter with Frankenstein's monster at a Niagara Falls wax museum, was always fascinated with ghosts, monsters, and things that go bump in the night.

In a story that was initially published in a small press U.S. magazine called the *Darker Woods* in 1997, and reprinted in my 2004 short story collection, *One Hand Screaming*, I explored this very concept.

"From Out of the Night" is a tale about a middle-aged writer of paranormal phenomenon; a man who has built his career on writing about monsters such as Bigfoot, The Loch Ness Monster, UFOs, and ghosts. (Sound familiar? Sometimes, the things writers do end up being an intriguing exercise in foreshadowing.) In any case, John, the main character in my story, is writing his latest book about the paranormal, and speculating on the reasons why people are so drawn to the shadows, to the things that go bump in the night, when he overhears a ruckus upstairs. His wife, Mary, has sent the kids downstairs to hide in the office where John is working hard to complete his book on time for his publisher, because she wants to keep them safe from the creatures that stalk the house when the sun goes down.

The story opens with a bit of writing from the introduction to John's book:

> Although technology dominates our world today, there still exist things that have been with us since we huddled in caves around brightly burning fires and avoided ominous shadows. Strange beings of the night become frighteningly real to us — even as we venture into the twenty-first century. Unknown things are still out there going bump in the night; a night where most of our dreams are nightmares. Scientifically, we have grown out of the dark ages, but our fears will forever remain among other frightened figures, jumping at shadows outside the cave.
>
> And perhaps for good reason....[1]

In the story, originally a tale of less than one thousand words, which I wrote the first draft of in the mid-1980s when I was in my mid-teens, I attempted to create a juxtaposition between rational science and paranormal or spiritual belief; imagining a near-future in which science and spirituality diverge even further apart, creating huge gaps between — gaps that are filled with fear and terror of the unknown. After all, the unknown, the things we aren't able to see, that which we cannot explain, is far more frightening.

INTRODUCTION

Over the years, the tale evolved as I kept re-writing the story. It was eventually published in 1997; but only after some excellent feedback from Editor Stephanie Connolly, who helped me draw out an element I had set up within the characters of John and Mary but hadn't yet properly formed. The story ended up being (without giving the ending away too much) about the fact that *we* are the monsters, through the things we choose to believe and the things we choose to ignore as we craft our lives.

Later in the story, learning a bit more about himself and his beloved wife, John composes the closing paragraph for the introduction to his book:

> Irritation occurs in the believer's heart when science or the reason of daylight find rational ways of knocking their beliefs and fears. But, given the fact that proving the non-existence of anything is virtually impossible, fears continue to haunt us. We are pursued from out of the night by dreams of the unknown and visions of the unexplainable — the unreal. Even if, one day, proof is given to us that our fear-created beings do not actually exist, we will probably invent new ones.[2]

I quite like this story — which has been with me since my teens — and was inspired by an incident that occurred in my home. My own fascination with fear and trying to understand why I ended up spending so much of my time writing stories that embraced the dark corners and that sought to lurk in the shadows is part of the reason; but so is the process and the manner by which the original eight hundred-word story evolved into something a little over two thousand words by the time it got published.

When I was first inspired to commit some words to paper, based upon a single scene that popped into my head, I had no idea the tale would evolve into something I could be truly proud of (thanks to that great editor); but also, no idea that the story would be quite so meta in nature, it being about a middle-aged writer working on books about the paranormal, a path that, thanks to Dundurn, I am quite enjoying.

Spooky Sudbury is another example of how something really great evolved out of a simple interaction; an unpredictable chain-reaction of events that, upon reflection, might have been the inevitable outcome.

My co-author, Jenny Jelen, wrote a bit about the experience in her column in the April 3, 2013, edition of *Northern Life*, talking about the specific instructions she was given, prior to conducting the interview, to figure out a way to localize the story about a book (*Haunted Hamilton*) centred on a town five hours away from Sudbury. During that interview, I spoke a bit about how I had always found the woods on the drive up Highway 144 to be a bit creepy; I also touched on the ubiquitous monster under my bed while growing up in Levack. The conversation led to her asking me if I had ever considered writing a similar book involving our hometown.[3]

We ended up sharing a few stories back and forth, and when Jenny began reciting tale after tale about local legends she had either researched already or had heard about, something clicked.

Why *hadn't* I written a book about hauntings and eerie phenomenon in the Sudbury area?

The practical, authorial part of me believed it was necessary to actually visit the places being written about, to personally experience the settings discussed, and meet some of the folks involved. I knew that writing a local book about my old hometown might be challenging. It would involve a great deal of

Introduction

The Big Nickel and Sudbury Superstack — two popular Sudbury signature landmarks.

travelling back and forth — easy enough, since my mom still lives in my childhood home in Levack, and there's always a place for me to stay and a personal reason to visit.

Certainly, part of the joy of writing *Haunted Hamilton* was going on the ghost walks and spending so much time with local "ghost busters" Daniel Cumerlato and Stephanie Lechniak, owners of Haunted Hamilton Ghost Walks & Events. I knew that much of what readers enjoyed in that book was the fact I wasn't just reporting details from afar; I had planted myself directly into the settings I was writing about, so I could describe them first hand. If I wanted to be true to the way in which *Haunted Hamilton* was conceived, researched, and written, I needed to do the same with the Sudbury book.

So, to be able to create a genuine, experiential appreciation for my beloved hometown in a relatively short period of time

— without having to be back there for every single element, or conduct each interview in person — I would need to collaborate.

And who better than the experienced journalist I was speaking with, who was as fascinated by the topic as myself?

The concept of writing a book of true stories about the Sudbury area lingered for several minutes, both of us enthusiastic, and it seemed natural for us to explore the concept of working on the book together. We parked the idea and completed the interview, agreeing to discuss it in more detail by phone, then again in person a couple of weeks later when I was visiting Sudbury.

At a Tim Hortons in New Sudbury we met in person for the first time, each having mapped out a few ideas on how we could put the book together. Combining Jenny's interviewing and reporting skills with my experience having already put together a book in this category, we sketched out an outline for how *Spooky Sudbury* could be broken up, how we could divide up the work, and what sorts of stories we were already familiar with that would help build out the tales involved.

From there, thanks to technology, it was a series of regular phone calls, texts, emails, Skype calls, and occasional coffee/breakfast/lunch meetings, when we were both available the same time in the same place, to complete the manuscript.

My publisher, Dundurn, was very receptive when I pitched the idea for *Spooky Sudbury*. Interested in publishing the book, the timing seemed to work such that, if Jenny and I were ready in time it could actually appear in the Fall 2013 catalog — just one year later. And, though I am a hybrid author, someone who has one foot firmly planted in traditional publishing while the other continues to explore the often more flexible and quick-moving landscape of self-publishing, I have to say that Dundurn has always been quick to react, fast to come to the support of an

INTRODUCTION

author, and have also done an amazing job of putting promotional opportunities in front of me — from local television and newspaper appearances to radio spots and local events at libraries, bookstores, and conferences. I adore working with them and admire the many elements they have created for their authors, such as the helpful and timely author newsletter, the detailed and informative author package they send out, and the regularly scheduled notifications about important dates regarding the author's publication.

In the creation of this book, Jenny and I took advantage of cloud-based storage via Google Drive to share the pieces we were each developing back and forth, along with cover concepts and photography discussions on what picture might work best with what story.

Throughout the process, I was reminded of the collaborative nature by which I had worked on the journal *Northern Fusion* that Carol Weekes and I co-edited while she was living in Ottawa, I in Hamilton, and the publisher in Montreal (this back when the internet was young and mostly involved text-based interactions).

Of course, with virtually every story or article that Jenny and I were developing, I couldn't help but harken back to my own childhood, to those aforementioned monsters, constantly drawing parallels from items we were working on to things I had experienced when I was a youth growing up in Levack.

While I cannot honestly say that I have ever seen a ghost, or a UFO, or any sort of actual monster other than the one I know still lives under my bed, I did spend a great deal of time in my childhood pursuing and focusing on the unknown.

There was one Halloween, for example, when I was perhaps eleven years old and there was a special on television about Bigfoot that I had seen advertised. The commercials

SPOOKY SUDBURY

for the program alone had given me nightmares (I have never pretended to be a brave person), and I was frustrated that it was airing during prime "trick or treat" time. So, despite being delighted to be out with my friends and gathering chocolate, candy and salty snack treats, I remember trying to look over the shoulders of the adults who were forking the candy over to see if I could catch a glimpse of the program on their television sets. In any home that did have that program on, I grilled the adults about what was happening. Remember, this was back at a time where there were 3 English language television programs available in Levack, before the wonders of "Cable" had arrived that far north. We had TVO, CTV, and CBC. So if a television was on and tuned to an English language station, there was a 33.33 percent chance (maybe even higher since CTV and CBC tended to be a bit more popular for most homes than TVO) that "Bigfoot" special was on.

Of course, grilling adults about mysteries was something I had already been comfortable with.

Inspired by a series of books that I couldn't get enough of when I was younger, the *Alfred Hitchcock and the Three Investigators* series, started by Robert Arthur Jr., I created a group of the same name and convinced my friend Steve Soulier, my cousin Michael Dusick, and his neighbour Robbie Abrams to join me.

The books centre on three teens (Jupiter Jones, Pete Crenshaw, and Bob Andrews) who solve crimes from a club-house (a trailer hidden under the junk pile in Jupiter's uncle's salvage yard and accessible via a hidden tunnel as well as an escape hatch). The three would solve crimes and also occasionally meet with famous director Alfred Hitchcock to review crime-solving techniques and seek advice. One thing I liked about the series was that the tales often suggested supernatural

INTRODUCTION

phenomenon, but the logical and analytical Jupiter Jones usually always found a way to explain away the ghosts using solid detective and Sherlock Holmes-style deduction. I adored the series, and, in my enthusiasm, wanted to solve crimes in the same way.

Robbie's mother had access to a printing press and so we had business cards created for our little team. And yes, there were four of us, but, being driven by the book series, I wanted us to be called the 3 investigators, just like the books. So we had Robbie listed as "Records & Research" (in the books, Jupiter did double duty for that role) while Mike, Steve and I were the investigators — poetic licence, then, for calling us 3 investigators (a habit I have continued well into my writing career).

There were only a couple of "cases" that we actually worked on in the small town of less than one thousand people. We rarely left Levack, the ward we all lived in — although I'm sure that the crimes being committed in the metropolitan centre of the city of Sudbury a 45-minute drive away would have given us a bit more content to investigate.

There was, as I recall, a robbery that took place at the local convenience store, the Mini Mart. The stolen and broken cash box was found in the woods not far from downtown Levack off Mine Road but the perpetrators were never found. Learning about this crime, and the evidence found, I dragged Michael, Steve, and Robbie along with me to scout the woods where the box was found looking for clues, footprints, torn bits of cloth, whatever we might be able to find. I also brought them with me as I knocked on doors of houses within sight of the Mini Mart and parts of Mine Road, handed the adults who answered those doors our business card and explaining who we were (just like the boys in the book did). I then asked the perplexed adults if they had seen or heard anything out of the ordinary on the date and time in question, and, sometimes, when the adults would actually humour me by providing an answer, I'd jot down anything they had to tell us in my handy spiral bound pocket notebook, then move on to the next house.

We, of course, never solved any crimes. The creative person in me might suggest that there were many unsolved mysteries still waiting to be cracked in my home town. We also likely confused a good number of adults by taking our imaginary play to the extreme. It's one things to play "cops and robbers." It's quite another thing to move beyond imaginary playground antics and into the real world, bringing innocent and unsuspecting adults along for the ride. My powerful young imagination, fueled by a love of reading, actually believed that a group of pre-teens could, if they put their minds to it, solve crimes just like Jupiter Jones, Pete Crenshaw, and Bob Andrews — after all, they were just three in a long line-up of youth crime-busters like the Hardy Boys, Nancy Drew and of course, Encyclopedia Brown. So why couldn't me and my friends do the same?

When I look back on this, I'm sure that I not only embarrassed my three friends into an activity that they weren't nearly as excited nor as passionate about as I had obviously been — but I do certainly appreciate how they must have worked hard to humour me in my outrageous endeavours.

When my wife Francine first heard about this motley young group I had organized, she did laugh, but she wasn't at all surprised. No, she knows me too well. I have long had a habit of being so bull-headed as to believe in something so strongly; typically something inspired by the written word.

I do, after all, even in my middle-aged years, continue to repeat the famous lesson learned by Spiderman "With great power comes great responsibility," like some personal mantra; even making sure my eight-year-old son is aware of the lesson that my writing hero, Stan Lee wrote in that legendary August

INTRODUCTION

1962 issue of *Amazing Fantasy #15* where Spidey made his first appearance. Not to mention that I can sometimes still be caught trying to be bitten by a spider on the off chance that it might help me gain the proportional strength, speed, and agility of the arachnid.

Besides trying to force my friends into the investigation of local crimes, I also spent time doing my own solo searches for Bigfoot, UFOs, and other proof that the monsters I had always imagined were indeed real.

I not only spent hours lying on my back and scanning the skies with my binoculars, in the hopes of spotting some sort of unidentified flying object, but I recall, one particular night in the mid-winter when, from my friend Troy Mallette's yard, I spotted what I thought was the Bigfoot creature walking up a snow-covered path at the end of Mountain Avenue.

Troy had just gone in for the night to his parent's home on Third Avenue; I was about to head home myself when I looked over and, about one hundred metres away, across a bit of a gulley and a creek, I saw a large dark creature lumbering up the hill and into the woods. He was moving in a strange way, taking huge, giant steps.

I shook my head, partially terrified, but also exhilarated by what I was witnessing.

Could this actually be Bigfoot, right there before me?

I strained my eyes, looked harder and, as the details re-settled themselves in my mind, I realized that what I was seeing was a person wearing a navy ski suit and toque, explaining the bulk. He was wearing skis, cross country skis, which I couldn't at first see from the distance, but which did explain the manner by which he was walking so strangely.

I stood there by myself in Troy's yard, watched as he reached the top of the small hill, then turned around and skied back down the short length of the knoll, then did it again, before heading off west-bound along the snow-covered path that ran alongside the creek.

As I stood there, my eyes casting out toward the path that led into the dark shadowed woods, I was inspired by that shock of fear I had felt and hoped that if I stood there long enough I would see some sort of Sasquatch creature coming out of the woods.

After a while, my feet cold and my head swimming with thoughts of all the hidden monsters stalking through the woods, I finally gave up and went home.

Other forest-related thrills I remember from my childhood involved stories that spread through our small town about the hermit who lived in the local woods. Parents warned us not to venture too far into the forest. This was something we did regularly — how could we resist, when there were so many great paths and wooded areas to explore. Levack, after all, was surrounded by thick lush forest on all sides — a veritable playground for anybody who loved the outdoors — not to mention anybody like me, who was convinced the woods were filled with supernatural beasties just waiting for me to discover.

But there were a few weeks where stories of this hermit kept us all on our toes, leading me to look a little more suspiciously at the woods. If there was indeed a homeless person living in the woods, it was very likely a person down on his luck who actually meant no harm to anybody. But that's the way stories and fears in a small town can easily spread. It was no different than that other time when there were stories of a white van stalking slowly through town, the strange man inside the van attempting to abduct local children. As kids, upon hearing these tales (likely simply local urban legends) we would run screaming whenever a white vehicle of any kind approached.

I recall when I was a bit older, hearing similar stories of

INTRODUCTION

someone in Dowling seen multiple times near twilight dressed up in a hunter's jacket and hockey mask, just like Jason in the *Friday the Thirteenth* movies. Those incidents inspired another story I had written entitled "Fall Spectacle" a tale that I haven't yet published anywhere but is indeed a tale set in and inspired by events from my hometown.

Speaking of the manner by which I would suspiciously eye the woods, I went on many fishing trips up Highway 144 with my father when I was young, and I always felt a little creeped out by the woods, by the tall trees that lurched up on either side of the highway, and of the secrets that those forests held.

I was so inspired by this experience that I did what I often do, I turned that inspiration into a story.

A tale I penned in my early twenties, entitled "Erratic Cycles" was published in a magazine that was produced right here in Sudbury. *Parsec* magazine, produced and edited by Sudbury's Chris Krejlgaard, featured science fiction from film, television, and literature. Chris published my story in the Winter 1998/1999 issue of *Parsec* alongside some beautiful artwork by Sandy Carruthers and with the sub-head to the story title reading: "A lonely stretch of highway takes one man back to a place he dreads."

Here is a short scene from the story that perhaps highlights the fear of those woods running alongside Highway 144 that have lingered with me my entire life:

> There was only quiet thought and gentle reflection as his car left the sprawling fringes of the city, headed north on Highway 400.
>
> And then, several hours later, the car — the very means of his pilgrimage — broke down.
>
> And Charles was alone.

In the middle of nowhere.

This newest development brought to him the real reason he had never let himself be alone for all those years.

Being alone scared the bejesus out of him

He was surrounded on all sides, it seemed, by the thick foliage of the Northern Ontario wilderness. Wilderness that grew darker as the sun crept down somewhere behind the distant hills.

Wilderness that threatened to take him back to when he was ten and camping with his parents at Algonquin Provincial Park.

Back to the last time he had really felt alone.

Back to the time when he had first learned of The Bush People.

"No," he whispered, and it all came back to him in a sudden rush, as if the nineteen years between today and that dreadful evening had never happened at all.

He was returned to that night — back inside the body of a ten-year-old who was alone and lost in the thick of the night in the middle of nowhere.

He experienced it all.

The cold chill of the night wind. The smell of the nearby lake which carried the faint scent of trout. The unending rhythm of the crickets, forever bleating their cries of passion for the night, their chant that there was much more to the darkness than could be seen.

And the knowledge, the dreadful, painful knowledge that his parents were still sleeping in the tent, completely unaware that he was no longer tucked in his sleeping bag, dozing peacefully and protected beside them.[4]

Introduction

There are so many elements from my childhood and youth that informed this story, and not just my fear of the woods that pressed in from either side of the barren and lonely stretches of Highway 144. The "Bush People" mentioned in this tale and associated with the eerie echos of loon calls that appear later in the same story, were derived from a tale that my friend J.P. Couvrette told when we were bunkmates working part-time on weekends during the school year at Fox Lake Lodge, which is located about an hour's drive from Cartier off Highway 144.

J.P. was a master storyteller, much like Laurie Blake, the lodge's owner back in the 80s when J.P. and I worked there alongside my best friend, John Ellis. Laurie Blake had a wonderful way of relaying beautifully crafted ghost stories around the camp fire. And J.P., a natural-born ham, also had that knack for telling fascinating tales and keeping a crowd of people huddled around to listen. This is a skill that he later adapted into the classroom, keeping students riveted and engaged in his Orillia area school. J.P. unfortunately succumbed to kidney cancer at the age of forty-one in August 2009 — before I ever had the chance to thank him for being such an inspiration to my writing, years after we had hung out together in our teens.

After hearing several creepy ghost stories told by Laurie, J.P. continued to share tales when we were back in our cabin, regaling me with stories such as the legend of "Old Crooked Neck," a lynched Indian chief whose spirit was carried by the call of the loon, seeking revenge on the descendants of the white men who murdered him and strung him up in a tree.

The combination of Laurie and J.P.'s storytelling mastery had me — even at the age of sixteen, when I was supposed to be brave and fearless in that teenage way — hiding under my sheets and gasping in fright every time I heard the haunting call of the loon echo out over Fox Lake. I lost a lot of sleep thanks to both

Spooky Sudbury

J.P. and Laurie — but I can now look back on those memories fondly and with an appreciation of the inspiration that they provided me.

Something else that I recall spending a great deal of time on, and this was in my senior year at high school, was the study of the Salem witch trials, which we had been learning about in grade thirteen history class; instead of doing a regular report for a presentation I was supposed to do in class, I created a music video.

Using the Rush song "Witch Hunt" from their 1981 album *Moving Pictures* as the audio track, I spent an evening with a bunch of friends in costumes, filming scenes involving a witch being chased through the woods by angry townspeople. For the additional cast members to help "flesh out" the mob scenes we even went to the Dairy Bar on Mine Road and asked anyone who had nothing to do if they wanted to be in the movie. We then drove back with them to the abandoned Warsaw area of Levack, the section of Levack that was closest to the mine — and where, even just five years earlier, houses had stood, — handed our volunteers torches, and set them about wandering down some forest and field paths with the torches ablaze.

I had attempted to follow Rush lyricist Neil Peart's lead by drawing a connection between the historical paranoia of the witch hunt and the paranoia of censoring theatre, movies, and books. As Peart wrote so eloquently in the song's lyrics, the thing to realize is how ignorance, prejudice, and fear work together.

The video is, of course, eerie and creepy, filled with dark images of a single witch running in terror as she is pursued by the angry mob bearing weapons and torches. The video includes flashes of books and magazines, including ones that were banned from sale in Canada (my teenage stand on censorship). The video ends with flashes of the witch (my good friend Steve Gaydos in

INTRODUCTION

costume) tied to a cross and howling in pain as she burns to death. It was meant to be, as Peart has suggested, an illustration of how the ignorant masses can be motivated to perform terrible acts and feed a mob mentality.[5]

As mentioned, and, as I hope to have illustrated by taking you back through a few specific scenes remembered from my youth in the town of Onaping Falls, I have always been inspired by fear and the unknown; and this has been a major factor in the types of things I have chosen to write about, including the co-authoring of this book with Jenny.

It started with that monster under my bed; but it continues with the monsters and creatures that I know still lurk in those dark shadows just out of sight.

As Hamlet explains so eloquently to his dear friend Horatio when the ghost of the young prince's father is seen skulking about in Shakespeare's famous play by saying that "there are more things in heaven and earth than are dreamt of in your philosophies," I, too, believe the same thing.

Sure, science, reason, and daylight can inform us that the things we are afraid of that lurk in the dark are merely figments of our imagination.

But they can never truly convince me that there isn't something else out there; that there isn't something which exists that, despite our science, despite our informed knowledge, we simply can't properly comprehend or understand.

And that is why, no matter how much light we might cast to dispel those shadows, there will always be the unknown, there will always be the fear of that we can't quite see but of which, occasionally, we catch a fleeting glimpse.

So, welcome to *Spooky Sudbury*, a book which is filled with page after page of those fleeting glimpses — something from the great beyond seen, heard, or felt momentarily, but enough

SPOOKY SUDBURY

to change the lives of the people affected; enough to open their minds into wondering what else is out there.

Sudbury is our home; a place where families have, since the late 1800s, felt safe to work, raise families, and enjoy building their lives. It is a place that many have tried to leave, but have been inextricably tied to. Consider folks like me, who first left in 1988, yet I am still drawn back.

But Sudbury is also a place with danger, and not just the danger that faces those brave enough to descend into the depths of the mines, or work the railways that were the first lifelines between our region and the rest of the world. Beyond those normal dangers lurk the fears that hide and flit among the many shadows; in the network of tunnels mined in the rock beneath our feet; in the buildings where we live and congregate to eat, enjoy the arts, and history; in the nearby woods that encase our city and town; in the rivers, streams, and bodies of water, and also in the skies above us.

Welcome to Sudbury. Stay, enjoy, curl up in a chair with this book and explore it, along with Jenny and I, pausing to take a second look at the mysterious, the unsettling, the unexpected, and the unexplained.

Mark Leslie
Sudbury, Ontario, 2013

Sudbury Spooks:
Ghosts, Spectres, and Other Apparitions

We Can't Be the Only Things Here

Mark Gregorini firmly believes "we can't be the only things here."

Perhaps that's why the restaurateur is so receptive to the strange presence that exists at his fine dining establishment on Kelly Lake Road.

The proprietor of Verdicchio Ristorante Enoteca said things have been a little less than normal "since the day we opened" in 1994. The early version of the presence was "a trickster," moving cutlery, turning them around, and causing teapots to fall. His mom, Willie, would get frustrated with staff for being careless in their table preparation.

"She would just think we didn't know to set the tables properly," Gregorini said with a laugh. Perhaps it was sometimes a staff member in a hurry — however Gregorini believes "it can't always be a figment of our imagination … Besides, you can only take that excuse so far."

In more recent years, the invisible being has ramped up its existence, exhibiting "more of a presence" at the restaurant.

SPOOKY SUDBURY

Or maybe it is other experiences Gregorini has had that made him more aware.

Sometime in the first half of the 2000s, Gregorini travelled back to his roots in Italy with his wife Laura. The two were in the southern region of Calabria, staying in a particular "old part of Italy."

Looking one direction, Gregorini had a breathtaking view of olive groves winding up the mountainous landscape. In the other direction was the ocean.

Gregorini and his wife were staying in the guest house of a family friend; the guest house was just two hundred meters from the main house.

When the couple first put their belongings into the guest house, they couldn't help but notice the odd décor. Gregorini vividly recalled a baby crib and a meat slicer pushed into the corner, along with pictures of Mary and Jesus hanging on the walls. The spiritual theme was prevalent during that particular trip — the two spent much of their time exploring monasteries in the old-time war zone. That's why when he dreamed of monks, he wasn't overly concerned.

He did, however, become uncomfortable after one sleepless night.

Both he and Laura had fallen asleep comfortably that memorable night. It wasn't until midway through the night that they were awoken.

"I felt something on my back," he said. "I think it's Laura. But I look, and she's on the other side of the bed."

He went to get her attention but, in that instant, Gregorini was paralyzed by the feeling of hands on his neck and leg.

Unable to move, he wanted nothing more than to get Laura's attention. From the grips of an unseen force, he was able to turn his head and watched as she sat up — straight up, arms outstretched, like Frankenstein.

48

We Can't Be the Only Things Here

"Turn on the light!" she said. "There's something in here."

The force let go of Gregorini, but fear of the unknown kept the two sleeping with the light on for the rest of the night.

The next day, Gregorini learned he wasn't the only one dreaming of men in cloaks — Laura had had similar dreams.

Not wanting to offend the gracious family that invited them to stay, the couple kept quiet about the experience. However, they did cut their visit short. When they returned home, Gregorini shared the incident with his brothers, who shed some light on the situation.

"History has it, behind the guest house in the forest, they had tried to excavate the land," Gregorini said. The rough terrain made it impossible though.

"When they tried to excavate, people died on it." Since then, others have refused to work on the land.

Having had an unquestionably real and unquestionably terrifying experience, Gregorini said the antics of the presence at the restaurant are purely playful, despite their more frequent occurrences.

"You get that feeling something is around," he said. One particularly noticeable event occurred in the banquet hall of the restaurant. Gregorini was sitting at a round table, chatting to two employees in the otherwise empty room. Set on the white tablecloth in front of them was an empty glass candleholder. The conversation came to a quick stop when the glass shattered to pieces right in front of their eyes.

Gregorini has never investigated why the place might be haunted. Instead, he opts to simply co-exist with the playful character. Staff members sometimes get a little "freaked out" by the presence, but Gregorini is certain it's nothing to worry about.

"I know it's there," he said. "If we exist as we are, how can that not exist?"

A Ghost He Couldn't Leave Behind[1]

During the Halloween season of 1999 — the time of year when many people are thinking about ghosts and goblins and other things that go bump in the night, an eighty-five-year-old Levack resident was more concerned about a ghost that never really left his mind.

Bruce Christie had written a book entitled *The Haunted House of Bruce Mine*, which was the true story of growing up in the town of Bruce Mines, situated less than a three-hour-drive from downtown Sudbury. Christie's book covered details about his childhood family house, where his family was accompanied by an unexpected permanent resident of the house they had nicknamed "Spooky."

The first appearance of this ghost occurred shortly after Bruce, his parents, and his seven siblings moved into the home in 1919. Spooky would mostly reveal himself to the family via a series of eerie nocturnal footsteps and creaking floorboards — something they got quite used to over the years.

Every once in a while Spooky would actually reveal himself to the family in the spectral guise of a man in a dark suit. He

A Ghost He Couldn't Leave Behind

would slowly materialize into existence right before them, and just as quickly fade from sight.

The first time that Spooky was heard in the home the family was a more than a bit frightened. But after realizing that the spectral resident of this home meant them no harm, they actually got used to him.

"If we heard something upstairs," Christie said, "we were more appeased to know it was the ghost and not a real person, a burglar."

In fact, during the Great Depression, a time when folks who were down on their luck and travelled as vagrants looking to either find shelter or steal food, Christie was propelled into a situation in which he had to aim a rifle out a second floor window to scare a vagrant off.

One wonders, of course, if the man had actually got into the house, if Spooky would have taken care of scaring him off all on his own.

In his writing and in an interview he gave to the *Sudbury Star* that was published in an October 25, 1999, article by Kennedy Gordon, entitled "Author in search of Spooky," Christie referred to a corner in the cellar where the cement had previously been dug up. He said that the house had burned down in 1934 and a new one had been put up over the old foundation; and that is where the truth about old Spooky still lies buried.

Christie made the trek into Sault Ste. Marie multiple times in order to dig through old town records from Bruce Mine, but was never able to find a reference to a cemetery or grave site on the property of his family's old home.

The new owners of the property even went so far as to extend an invitation to Christie to visit, take photographs, and examine the property in his quest. But nothing ever did come of it, leaving Christie with that one last chapter from his book unresolved.

SPOOKY SUDBURY

"I'm sure there's a body under there," Christie said, when reflecting on what might exist under the old cellar floor of his old house.

Unfortunately, he never got to find out.

That, of course, didn't prevent Spooky from still haunting his memory, like thoughts and cherished recollections of a dear childhood friend.

If only all of our ghosts could come with such fond memories.

HAUNTED 2650 LEVEl OF LEVACK MINE

It is a well-known fact that shift work and general over-tiredness can often lead to a change in perception, a blurring of the lines between reality and the dream world. In his 1996 book, *Sleep Thieves*, Stanley Coren described the effects of sleep-deprivation on our physical and mental health.

One such side-effect has to do with hallucinations. Coren documented what happened when Peter Tripp, a New York City DJ, decided to go without sleep for two hundred hours for a charity fund-raising event.[2] Early into the experience, Tripp experienced distortions in his visual perceptions: he was interpreting spots on the table as bugs, seeing spiders crawling around his booth, and even spinning webs on his shoes.[3] Later on, Tripp was so susceptible to delusions that he became convinced that the doctor monitoring his health was actually an undertaker there to bury him alive. Tripp could no longer properly distinguish between reality and his nightmares.[4]

Tripp's experiences are perhaps a bit extreme, but Coren also includes multiple references to the effect of shift-work on internal circadian clocks. He illustrates how workers on rotating shifts tend

SPOOKY SUDBURY

to sleep two less hours per day, spend most of their time sleeping in the lightest stages of sleep, and thus typically suffer from sleep deprivation and build up a significant amount of sleep debt.[5]

Combine Coren's findings regarding the effect of twelve-hour shift-work with being alone in a dark, damp, cold place and you can just imagine how it would wreak havoc on a person's imagination.

That's exactly the type of thing that Sudbury area historian Hans Brasch, author of multiple books about mining in the Sudbury area, including *Levack Mine: 100 Years (1912 to 2012)*, might tell you when sharing a particular ghost story.

"The mine used to be closed on the weekend. The mine was entirely empty on weekends back then except for emergencies," Hans Brasch said over a coffee at the Tim Hortons in Dowling. "The only people around would be a single hoistman, one operating shaft boss (OSB), and one fireguard."

Brasch explained that the fireguard would have to climb down the ladder, travel throughout the mine, and occasionally punch a clock to certify that he had visited particular locations. At the end of each trip the fireguard would get into the cage and be hoisted back up to the surface.

On one lonely night in the mid 1970s the operating shaft boss received a phone call from the 2650 level. It was the fireguard, entirely panic-stricken.

"Get me out of here!" the fireguard screamed.

"What's wrong?"

"I need to get out of here! Now!" he pleaded. The OSB could hear the terror in the man's voice and paused to ask if he was injured or if there had been some sort of accident.

"No," was the response. "I'm not hurt. Get me up! Now!"

The cage, which travelled at fifteen hundred feet per minute, took almost fifteen minutes to bring the fireguard up. The

Haunted 2650 Level of Levack Mine

hoistman needed to do a trial trip first, which would add about five or six minutes to the overall journey. The whole time he was waiting, the operating shaft boss was worried for the safety and well-being of the fireguard. He also wondered if, by the time the cage arrived, the fireguard would be "over" the incident in question. But despite the length of time it took to get up, the fireguard arrived still terrified. He was visibly shaken and the panic in his voice hadn't subsided.

"There's someone down there!" the fireguard said.

"You're the only one down there."

"No, there is someone! Some *thing* is down there! A ghost! I saw a ghost down there!" the fireguard insisted.

"There's no such thing," the OSB replied. "Settle down. You're fine."

"I'm not fine! I was down there in the dark with a ghost."

There was nothing that the operating shaft boss nor the hoistman could do to alleviate the fireguard's angst over what he had seen. He went on to swear on a stack of Bibles that he had seen a ghost on 2650 level.

Hans Brasch explained that he had been fireguard multiple times but he himself had never seen a ghost. However, despite not believing in ghosts, he enjoys sharing a ghost story or two of his own and understands just how much fear belief in ghosts can strike in men's hearts.

He relayed a tale passed down from his grandfather about a dare several millwrights made with one another one night while drinking. The dare involved taking a stake and driving it into the soil of a recently filled nearby grave which was a short walk through the woods. Finally stealing up his courage, the one millwright went off alone into the woods to perform his dare. He never returned, and the men assumed that he had chickened out and gone home. The next morning, they found him, dead and

On one lonely night in the mid 1970s, the operating shaft boss received a phone call from the 2650 level. It was the fireguard, entirely panic-stricken.

lying on top of the grave right beside where he had driven the stake into the ground. When the scene was investigated, they determined that the man had driven the stake into the ground, just like he had been dared, but hadn't noticed that he had driven the stake right through his own apron, thus rooting himself to the spot. When he tried to leave, he felt himself being pulled and held there, and the shock of believing that it was a ghost holding him there is what killed him. Brasch's grandfather's tale is a wonderful classic tale of graves, stakes, and aprons, and one told many times over the years and from different locales, but is certainly an enjoyable one to hear, because it draws upon a universal truth — the ultimate power of fear.

Hans then told another story from his grandfather, regarding a stable boy sleeping in the hay who swore he had woken up in the middle of the night to see a ghost milking the cows. Terrified, the stable boy refused to stay in the stables. Hans's grandfather calmed him down and decided to stay with him the following night to investigate the situation and put his fears at ease. Surely the boy had been the victim of an over-active imagination. Sure enough, under the light of the moon, a white spectre appeared in the barn and proceeded to walk over to the cows with a bucket and begin the task of milking. Hans's grandfather snuck up behind the ghost and tossed a bucket of water onto the figure. He then pulled the white soaked sheet off of the figure's head. It wasn't a ghost after all, but a neighbour, sneaking in the middle of the night to steal milk.

Hans talked about his admiration for a fun ghost story, explaining that he felt most really good ghost stories begin with a kernel of truth, but that they are often peppered with a fierce imagination, often one that is fueled by fear; and not just the fear of the person who experienced the incident, but also fear in the listener's heart.

When asked about whether or not that particular fireguard might have actually seen something paranormal on 2650 Level at Levack Mine, Brasch went on to explain what he thought might have happened.

"I think he really *did* see something." Brasch said. "And he is convinced that what he saw was a ghost. But here is what I believe he really saw."

Brasch explained that sometimes a cat, racoon, or other nocturnal animal would climb into the timbers on the trucks and get hauled down into the depths of the mine. Once transported underground, the animals would wander around, panicked and confused.

He also said that sometimes bats would find themselves down in the deep dark shafts. "Bats can be good," Brasch says, explaining he had a friend who suggested he leave a bat in his own attic one time, because they eat all the insects.

Spooky Sudbury

"But in a mine, a bat hanging down from the ceiling could sometimes spook people."

When the fireguard was walking around and shining his light to inspect the mine, Brasch believes that what he most likely saw, when he claimed to have seen a ghost, is the reflected light in the eyes of a small animal peeking out from the dark.

Two eerie looking eyes staring back at the fireguard.

His ghost.

At least that is what Hans Brasch believes. He smiles and jokes and says that you never really know.

The fireguard was not so easily convinced. He continued to swear that 2650 Level was haunted and that he had been down there alone with a ghost that evening and he swore that he would never go back down.

He never did go back underground again.

Sydney Brown's Undying Passion for the Theatre

Theatres are where stories come to life. Since it first began staging shows in September 1982, the Sudbury Theatre Centre (STC) stage has seen it all: dramas, comedies, tragedies, musicals, and more. However, that was hardly the beginning. The theatre had been putting on performances for more than a decade before it took up permanent residency on Shaughnessy Street in downtown Sudbury. It would "borrow" space at Laurentian University, Cambrian College, and even the old Inco Club in order to get actors on stages and audiences in seats.

It all began when the Ontario Arts Council and the Canada Council for the Arts put out *The Awkward Stage*, a book that outlined the findings of a 1967 theatre study. One of the recommendations put forward was for Sudbury to have a permanent professional theatre. Barrie's Gryphon Theatre Co. approached local amateur groups for sponsorships of a production, but the groups declined. Some enterprising Sudburians from each of the groups, however, thought it was a worthwhile risk. That's when Sonja Dunn, Carolyn Fouriezos, Bill Hart, Bob Remnant, and Peg Roberts began raising funds to bring the talented young Barrie company to Sudbury for a production of Neil Simon's *Come Blow Your Horn*. Joe Skerry and George Bernie MacMillan were added to the committee as treasurer and social convenor respectively.

The show was not only an artistic success, but a financial one too. Audiences responded positively, saying they would be more than happy to support a permanent professional theatre in Sudbury. That was all the encouragement the group needed to continue pursuing a pro company on home soil. Morey Speigal became the committee's first chairman in July 1971.

The official creation of the theatre is described on the organization's website, "Letters patent incorporating Sudbury Theatre Centre were granted on September 14, 1971, and Sudbury Theatre Centre was born."

The early years weren't necessarily all sold-out shows, but the board of directors was always looking for ways to improve. It didn't take long before the STC had gained experience, national notice, and a certainty that the theatre was here to stay.

By the mid 1970s, season subscriptions had tripled, and an increasing number of performances were sold out. By 1977 the seating capacity at the Inco Club had increased to 245 and each show was running for ten evening performances. This was about the time Sydney Brown became affiliated with the story of the STC.

The STC was still finding its permanent home when Brown began his stint with the theatre. The Englishman had originally come to Canada when he was fifteen. A year after arriving in Canada, he enlisted. Once he left the army, he decided to pursue his passion — acting.

"I was discharged in Toronto ... took drama lessons and set out to stun Broadway with my tremendous talent, which failed to impress the Yanks, who had no use at the time for strange young English actors," he was quoted as saying in a *Montreal Gazette* article published March 3, 1979.

Sydney Brown's Undying Passion for the Theatre

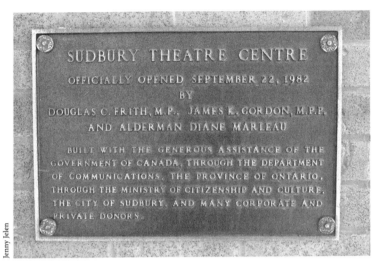

Even though he never did see the theatre open at its current Shaughnessy Street location, Albert said Brown's spirit followed the rest of the STC crew when it made the move.

Although Broadway frowned upon his accent, Brown worked in film and television for several decades before coming on board with the Sudbury Theatre Centre. He would have been part of nine STC shows, had he made it to the opening night of *Artichoke*.

It was 1979 when STC's long-time artistic director Tony Lloyd was gearing up for the opening night. *Artichoke* was the story of a Saskatchewan family making the best of their prairie existence. Brown was rehearsing for the role of Gramps along with the rest of the cast at the old Canada Bread factory on King Street.

He didn't make it to the first curtain though. Brown was eighty years old when he passed away suddenly of a heart attack.

"He just didn't come in that one morning," said Albert (not his real name), a former STC employee.

While Albert only began working at the theatre after Brown passed away, he was no stranger to the stories. Anytime

SPOOKY SUDBURY

something out of the ordinary would happen, everyone thought of Brown first. Strange sounds and missing props were often attributed to him.

"Oh, that's Sydney," Albert said. "We used to joke about it all the time." While he was handed blame for slight misfortunes, it wasn't always bad news when Brown was around. It's been said he has been responsible for a pleasant surprise or two since taking up residency at the theatre.

Even though he never did see the theatre open at its current Shaughnessy Street location, Albert believes Brown's spirit followed the rest of the STC crew when it made the move.

"He kind of moved over when we moved to the theatre centre ... He moved with us."

Albert has never seen the ghost himself, but others claim to have laid eyes on a mysterious figure floating around the theatre from time to time.

WANAPITEI'S NORTH RIVER GRAVEYARD

Joanne and her husband had long been blessed with being able to enjoy the wilderness of the Wanapitei area. After growing up in the area, the pair wed and began their married life there, enjoying the natural beauty of the sandy plains, the luscious streams, and the gently rolling rocky land that the Wanapitei Provincial Park offered.

At times, when they felt a little like being adventurous, they would walk at night. On one particular night back in the summer of 1994, their midnight walk took them on a visit to an old gravesite at the North River — a gravesite that has been there for a long time, as evidenced by the crosses dating back as early as the 1800s.

"One night," Joanne recalled, "we were all sitting at the campfire and decided to go pay a visit to the dead."

It was a beautiful night, the full moon cast rich light down upon the camping friends and stars twinkled in the black sky, almost winking at them as they planned their adventure. The road to the old cemetery was long and spooky, with the tall trees blocking much of the ambient light being cast down from the moon.

"There were about six of us," Joanne said. "Three couples, all with beers in hand, walking with our flash lights to our creepy destination." Finally, after what seemed like ages, they arrived and spied the first grave, a crib made out of old wood and a cross on top of it dated 1802, and marked with a little girl's name.

A collective shiver ran up the spines of the three couples before, without speaking, they walked on. There was something about the grave that stirred something up in all of them, a profound sadness, but also the feeling that something just wasn't right. And though nobody spoke about it then, Joanne later expressed the feeling that everybody was reacting to, that they were affected by a presence that none of them could explain.

As they walked on through the graveyard, continuing to explore, they noted the uneven ground. Soft in some spots yet bumpy in others; they found it difficult to navigate the terrain in the dark.

"At this point," Joanne said, "My arms and legs were shaking, and all I wanted to do was leave as soon as possible." It was the first time she had ever visited the graveyard, and she was having second thoughts about the group's desire to make their trek that night.

"With a beer in hand and my husband's arm in the other, we slowly walked along. Our flashlights were flickering and getting weaker by the second."

Oh my god, Joanne thought, *what if all their lights went out*!

As if on cue, their flashlights all went out at almost the exact same time.

That clinched it for the group. One of the others, Joanne wasn't sure who, let out a harsh gasp of fright and they all started running back toward the campsite, ignoring the treacherous landscape that they had previously negotiated with such care.

Wanapetei's North River Graveyard

"Lady Forgotten" — *Conceptual Graveyard Ghost Photo.*

It felt as if there was a presence in the forest — something ominous. The entire group couldn't put enough distance between themselves and the old graveyard.

"Thank goodness for the moon," Joanne said when thinking about their sudden flight. "We started running back toward the camp, real fast. My heart was beating profusely."

After finally arriving at the campfire, completely unharmed, they stood around breathless and silent. Being back at their campsite, with the fire burning strongly, the familiar setting, and their outdoor possessions nearby, the feeling of dread turned to laughter.

They had a few more beers and ended up laughing the rest of that night.

Throughout the years, Joanne and her husband returned to the graveyard, but only during the day. Each and every time

Spooky Sudbury

they visited, the land and crosses would be increasingly damaged by vandalism.

Joanne felt bad for the people buried at the graveyard; they seem to have been forgotten by time, but not left unmolested by vandals.

"Maybe that is why our flashlights all went out that night." Joanne said. "Maybe the graveyard was protecting itself from us."

Joanne says that you cannot even tell it is a graveyard anymore. The baby's crib has been destroyed; all that is left is a small cross and some broken pieces of wood on the ground.

"All in all," Joanne said, "I heard many stories of campers who were haunted by the spirits of this graveyard. He who has destroyed it, shall have many more spooky tales to tell…"

Stay Away From Joe Lone's Place

The following tale is a story sent to us from Halifax author Steve Vernon. Steve, who is often referred to as Halifax's hardest-working horror writer, is perhaps one of the most prolific genre writers in Canada. He has published hundreds of short stories in magazines and anthologies around the world, has about a dozen books out from various local speciality presses and regional publishers, and is also authoring a hot-selling serialized YA thriller ebook series called *Flash Virus*.

Steve calls himself a storyteller, and for good reason. He is a master of delivering oral tales; anybody who has ever had the pleasure of watching him take command of a live audience while doing a talk or reading knows the type of power that spoken word stories can have on a crowd when done by the right person.

Crediting his grandfather with teaching him the art of storytelling, Steve teaches the tradition to Nova Scotia children as part of their Writers in Schools program. He has four ghost story collections — including *Halifax Haunts, Haunted Harbours: Ghost Stories from Old Nova Scotia* and *The Lunenburg Werewolf and*

Spooky Sudbury

Other Stories of the Supernatural, both available in traditional print format and on ebook.

Although Steve has lived in Halifax for nearly forty years, his earliest formative years were spent in Capreol. When Steve was chatting with Mark about this book, he was pleased to be able to share a tale from his own childhood, an eerie memory of something that sent shivers down the spine of him and his neighbourhood friends.

There is an old dirt road that snakes into the woods just behind the C.R. Judd Public School.

Actually, it is more of a semi-ambitious rut through the bush rather than an actual dirt road. It sort of looks like a path had been trod down by a drunken senile moose. If you follow it you will come to a clearing, usually filled with tall dry grass and a scatter of wildflowers.

It is pretty in the summer. Devil's paintbrush, shocks of purple thistle, and tall wavering purple spires of fireweed trembling in the hot August wind.

There are two cabins in that field.

The one furthest from the dirt road is actually an old abandoned farmhouse. A French-Canadian family lived there for a few years with a small farm with a very large pig, a few fat geese, some worried-looking chickens, a horse that looked as if it might have run off from a glue factory and a couple of ill-bred dogs — along with about six or eight kids.

The cabin closest to the mouth of the dirt road is the one that everyone in our town called Joe Lone's cabin.

Joe Lone was reputed to have been a hermit who lived for years alone in that cabin. He was said to have been a karate expert who could break baseball bats over his own back.

Stay Away From Joe Lone's Place

I remember as a kid being puzzled at the notion of how a man would possibly break a baseball bat over his backbone. Would he tuck it under his elbows and snap the bat in two — using his back as a lever?

Or would he just Babe Ruth it backwards over his shoulder blades?

Like I said, it was a mystery.

It was definitely puzzling.

Every kid in that high school knew of that cabin and talked of how Joe Lone had hung himself in that cabin one lonely, cold winter night.

"He used a rope that he braided from his own hair," some kids said.

I had tried that myself.

Not hanging, you understand — but braiding a rope from my own hair.

I didn't get so much as a thread's worth out of the entire process — so I have since dismissed that embellishment as a rural urban myth.

For myself I figured that he had probably just snapped a baseball bat one too many times against his back bone and had inadvertently impaled himself with a shard of Louisville Slugger.

I imagined how he had felt at that time — lying in there on the uncarpeted pine floorboards of his cabin, bleeding to death with a deadly looking splinter of Slugger stuck between his shoulder blades. It might even have severed his spinal cord so he wouldn't have been able to crawl anywhere for help.

Might be he was too embarrassed to even make the attempt.

The kids of our school all swore that the ghost of Joe Lone still haunted that cabin and that on certain moonlit nights the walls of the cabin would shiver and shake and shudder — even when there wasn't a breath of wind to be found.

Spooky Sudbury

The family that had lived briefly in that other cabin spoke of seeing strange lights and hearing strange moaning sounds. They could have easily claimed that cabin as their own. No one really owned that land or that cabin — as far as anyone knew — but they preferred to stay away from that cabin.

"It smells funny in there," the father told me. "Like it don't feel right."

It became a dare and a bet amongst us kids to spend a night in that cabin — but so far as I know there wasn't a single kid in our little railroad town who found the nerve to actually spend the night.

I actually did visit that cabin in the daytime one summer — long after the French-Canadian family had moved away, pig, horse, geese, chickens, children and all.

I was about sixteen years old at that time.

The door of that cabin was broken and hung open, like the gaping mouth of a dead man.

The room was hot and close. I could smell old sawdust and must and about forty or fifty years' worth of accumulated funk.

I sat on the floor.

I listened for a while.

I did not hear a moan nor shudder nor even the rattle of a chain — but I felt as if someone was watching me the whole time.

There was a stain on the floor boards.

I was not sure whether it was blood or rain or somebody's last cup of coffee.

I ran my fingers over the floor boards, idly teasing them around the border of that stain.

I remember my fingertips tingling, as if I were running them through some sort of electronic field.

Just then the wind slammed that broken door shut.

SLAM!

Stay Away From Joe Lone's Place

I jumped and I ran.

I left that cabin on the double with the door hung half-open.

Some nights I'll sit up in bed — almost forty years later.

I can still hear the slamming of that broken cabin door.

It sounded a little like a baseball bat, slamming a man's backbone.

As far as I know that cabin's out there still.

Stay away from Joe Lone's place.

CHARLIE SMITH'S GHOST

Charlie Smith lives in a haunted farmhouse in Massey, part of the Sables-Spanish township in the Sudbury District, approximately seventy-five kilometres southwest of central Sudbury.

Charlie Smith was born in Blind River in 1948 and, the son of an ex-marine father, moved with his family regularly during his childhood. As a result, he attended seven different public schools, a challenging enough circumstance for a child. But, as an additional hardship, Smith was also diagnosed with dyslexia. Professionals told Smith's mother that he would never learn to read or write.

Becoming a renowned writer, poet, and storyteller who has captivated audiences for years, he certainly showed them!

Smith began composing poetry shortly after a near-death experience at the age of eight, and has been writing ever since. When he was eight years old, Smith's appendix ruptured, and his memories from that period are widely varied: from sitting on his father's knee reading a Tarzan comic book, to hovering above a scene featuring his father holding his lifeless form in a hospital waiting room, him being placed on a gurney and hospital

CHARLIE SMITH'S GHOST

workers in white jackets "pumping away" at him before he again regained consciousness. Smith amusedly says that the experience wasn't scary, but pleasant and that it eased the fear of death in him.[6]

When prompted for writing advice, his conviction is strong, but his advice is pure and straightforward. "I carry a small pocketbook," he says, explaining it as the place where most of his poems start. Smith goes on to explain that, because, everybody has ideas that flash quickly into their mind, using that pocketbook to capture those fleeting ideas and inspirations is important. "When they come, you have to chain them to the paper or they get away."[7]

He is not the type of person to take "no" for an answer, particularly not when it is something he is passionate about. Having worked as a farmer and a miner for Rio, Algoma, and Inco, Smith decided to leave mining behind after a second near-death experience in which he slammed into a signal light so hard that it destroyed his helmet and left him with a concussion. This was followed by the tragic death of a co-worker at a uranium mine near Elliot Lake just a few months later.[8]

In 1979, Smith and his wife Rhonda (a woman he still speaks of in the manner of the teenager who first fell in love with her almost five decades earlier) bought a farmhouse that they christened with the name "Earthfast" due to the fact that, as Smith says, "Nothing seems to leave this place."[9]

Smith is a councillor for the Township of Sable-Spanish River and he and his wife Rhonda have three children and five grandchildren.

Among Smith's other "children" are his books and CDs. In addition to the occasional magazine article and newspaper column, Smith has written two books of poetry, *The Beast that God Has Kissed* and *Through Three Long Miles of Night*; a book of short stories, *Tag Adler Tales*; and recorded a spoken word CD, all published by Scrivener Press in Sudbury. Charlie Angus has also used one of his poems as song lyrics on one of his CDs and Jeff Wiseman has used many of them on a CD called *Silvereyes*.

Smith's writing focuses on the things he loves: farming,

Charlie Smith began composing poetry shortly after a near-death experience at the age of eight, and has been writing ever since.

hunting, and the people of his beloved Northern Ontario. Supernatural elements arise in Smith's writing as an expression of the intimacy that people who work dangerous jobs, such as farmers, miners, and hunters (roles Smith is intimately familiar with), have with death.

Given Smith's legacy as a storyteller, we are sure you'll agree the best way to experience the thrill of his prose and poetry is directly through Charlie's words. His untitled story, which we fondly call "Charlie Smith's Ghost", and his poem "Runoff" both inspired by Smith's actual experiences, appear below.

CHARLIE SMITH'S GHOST
BY CHARLIE SMITH

I haven't seen him for a long time now. The last time I saw him, I was looking down into the cellar to see if the dirt floor was flooding from the rain. He was standing at the bottom of the "Finlander" type stairs, and was reaching up to the floor joist after something, something I suppose that he had stored there a century or so before. Then he was gone.

He never made a big show of himself, not ever, not like the little girl poltergeist. He was no child but a farmer — the man that built all this and I hope that even if no more Traceys live here he is happy enough with me. Mostly I just caught glimpses of him when doing things, sort of like a shadow passing on the periphery of my vision, but once or twice he came right out in the open.

I was haying, back in the days of square bales; I had a couple of the teenage boys in the neighbourhood working for me and it was hot. We had eaten and were still sitting around the long table — those boys, my daughter and son who were about the same age, and of course my wife and I. Apparently Tracey thought we were taking too long. Maybe we were, but it was hot, and those kids had worked hard. I could see no harm in letting them sit in the cool of the old farmhouse kitchen for a while longer.

He came striding out of the piano room dressed in grey. Everything about him was grey. He didn't even look at us but reached up where the hats were hung by the door, took his down — it had appeared as suddenly as Tracey — put it on, opened the door, and went out, closing the door firmly behind him.

"Who was that?" said somebody.

"Matt?" answered someone else, (Matt was the only guy not still at the table).

I smiled. I knew who it was, "It wasn't Matt!"

"Well who else could it have been?"

I think that most of us had seen Tracey, but their minds were sort of slipping around his existence. "Matt!" his brother David yelled.

"What?" came Matt's voice from upstairs in the washroom that my father-in-law had installed.

All the young folks were looking at each other, "It was a ghost!" I said, "Old Tracey."

"Jim Tracey?" my wife asked.

"No, I think it is his father — the old man who died in this house and was here for days until the neighbours all got together and shoveled a road out through the drifts. Some were so big that they had to tunnel through them." I nodded. "That's who it was."

There are other ghosts in this house, or there used to be. They have been getting fainter all the time. Jim visited the night he died in the hospital far away. I sensed him in the washroom (that used to be his bedroom), and later that evening, out at the barn. I never saw his apparition and I would even guess that someone with no Celtic heritage might not have noticed his chilly presence at all, but then I did not even know he was sick,

CHARLIE SMITH'S GHOST

let alone the fact that he had passed over.

Then there is Jim's sister the sickly child who died at twelve or so and liked to play noisy tricks. I have written lots about her. Her hijinks, her tinkled visitations, her swiping of small object, and her reintroductions of these things at the most inopportune times. But she has faded away to only a memory now too.

Where do they go — these ghostly friends? Do they fade into oblivion? Do they at last find paradise or purgatory, or perhaps they had already done this and this was the home for their ka and at last it passed on?

I do not have an answer for any of these things but I miss them now that I do not see them anymore. I hope they are well and not just whirling in the sour winds of oblivion.

I named this place Earthfast because of them and when people would ask me, "Are you not afraid there?"

I would answer, "Why would I be afraid of those fine people?"

"Well, what about when you are alone?"

I would smile and say, "But you see, I am never alone."

Runoff
By Charlie Smith

(From *The Beast That God Has Kissed*[10])

Water through snow, when it runs in the spring
Is attractive to children as near anything,
And I have to admit, if asked, "Is it fun?"
That even I like to make spring water run;
So I dig out the culvert under the lane,
Then next year I figure I'll do it again.

 I was knee-deep in March, wet slush and pleasure,
I would shovel a bit, then watch at my leisure —
The water was running, giggling snow
Soaked in the slush, then slobbering slow
Seeping along over grass from last year,
Then sucked in the culvert and foaming like beer.

 My gray house with its history was dreaming above
Of long lilting lifetimes of labour and love
For the land where I'm steward, was farmed here before —

Runoff

How many farmers have smiled at this chore?
For the earth, wind and water will seep in your soul,
And this is one rite that ties up the whole.

My son and a friend, when driving by greet me.
I wave back at them, but they're not going to cheat me;
It's just once a year and those two teenage boys
Can go off and play with their more modern toys.
But when they came back (I was dry in my home)
They asked, "Where is Brandon?" — but I was alone.

"Then who was that child who was helping you there,
With his feet in the water, with wind in his hair?
He puddled in puddles, and trenched with his toe."
They both clearly saw him — I really don't know,
A lost little ghost from the house on the hill?
I didn't see him (I did feel a thrill);

And I did feel a presence a couple of times
Like the long shivered tinkle of distant wind chimes…
Water through snow when it runs in the spring
Is attractive to children as near anything:
The earth, wind and water will seep in your soul,
And this is one rite that ties up the whole.

THE MAN SHE NEVER MET

Brianne Gagnon was about three years old when her parents showed her a picture of her late grandfather Bertrand Gagnon.

The small-town horseman had passed away April 18, 1995, at 3:00 p.m. One month later, right down to the hour, Brianne was born. The Chelmsford girl was never able to meet her grandfather, but always seemed to share a connection with him.

When her parents showed her the photo, her response shocked them.

"I told them I knew who he was," she recalled. "I said 'He was my grandpa that played the accordion when I went to bed.'"

Her parents looked at her in awe, as Bertrand was quite proficient on the instrument. Of course, Brianne would have had no way of knowing this.

Since then, Brianne has always felt affection for the man she never met. When she had the chance to buy a horse of her own, she couldn't help but think of Bertrand again.

"His horses meant the world to him," she said. "He loved horses — especially black ones."

THE MAN SHE NEVER MET

Her equine shopping trip led her to a big, black, standard bred horse named Bert. He had been successful on the racetrack before he moved on to become a pleasure riding horse. As soon as she heard the horse's name, she knew he would be hers.

"My grandpa is the reason I bought Bert," she said. "Same name, black horse."

Reassuring Encounters

Sometimes the supernatural can be a blessing. Lise Bertrand said the regular visits she gets from her grandfather are the most reassuring encounters she has ever experienced. She appreciates them so much that she wishes everyone could be as fortunate.

The local musician currently resides in the house her grandmother and grandfather built in 1934. She shares the old Capreol home with her husband.

The first time Lise met the ghost of her grandfather was after her life "was turned upside down" by a car accident. A serious shoulder injury kept her from her passion — playing the guitar. It also prevented her from working as a personal support worker.

"I could barely keep care of myself, let alone someone else," she said. "There were many dark days."

She was sound asleep one night, during that particularly trying period of time, when a force woke her up. She looked around the room before her eyes fell on the shape of a man standing in front of her window, next to her bed.

"I recognized this figure as my grandfather who had died in 1970," she said. "He was dressed in a long coat and wore a suit and a fedora. I didn't know if I was dreaming or hallucinating from the pain medication that I was on, but his presence made me feel at peace.

"He didn't speak but somehow I knew that he was there to look out for me. He stood there for a few minutes then he was gone."

Lise couldn't shake the experience from her head. She wanted to tell someone, but she didn't want to tell her husband because he is afraid of the paranormal. She tried to keep it to herself, but it soon became too much to handle.

"After a few days, I finally had to tell him what had happened that night because I couldn't stop thinking about it," she said. "As he listened, he started to smile and told me that he had seen my grandfather, too, but he wasn't 'spooked' about it. I was elated that it wasn't all in my head; my grandfather did come to visit us."

Since then, Lise's grandfather has returned a number of times. The most recent experience occurred just before Christmas 2012.

"I was wrapping gifts at the kitchen table and I saw him walk toward my curio cabinet in the living room," Lise recalled. "I later looked at the cabinet and realized everything was moved on the top shelf but no other shelves were touched.

"I have a collection of ceramic guitars that are always on display in the same way, but now they were moved into the corners of opposite sides of the shelf. I put them back to where they were supposed to be."

However, Grandpa seemed to have his own preference about where the guitars should go.

"A few days later it had happened again," Lise said. "The top shelf was the only one that was touched and once again the guitars where moved to opposite corners. I jokingly said 'Okay Grandpa. I don't mind when you come and visit us, but please stop moving my guitars around.'"

Spooky Sudbury

The guitars haven't been touched since. Lise still, however, likes knowing her grandfather is near.

"I like the fact the every once in a while my grandfather comes and checks in on me," she said. "I look forward to his visits. I wish everyone could be as fortunate as I am."

CINDY'S GUARDIAN ANGEL

There is an unquestionable energy inside Crumbz Bakery. As far as the owner, Cindy Babcock, is concerned, it's because her "guardian angel" has never left her side.

In life, Susan Vaillancourt was Cindy's right-hand woman. She was in line to manage the bakery, until a terminal cancer diagnosis interrupted their plans. Susan passed away May 3, 2012.

"She was an amazing friend," Cindy said. "She loved being at the bakery and was excellent at decorating cakes."

Suzy, as she was known, was also a big part in Cindy's successful start-up.

"She knows what I went through to get it going," Cindy said. "It's tough to start a business when (the town has) been on strike for almost a year." (Cindy is referring to the Vale mine strike, July 2009–July 2010.)

That's why when Cindy's employees told her about the strange events taking place in her shop, she was comforted.

One morning, her unsettled bakers informed her that the doorbell in the front of the store had chimed off, but no one had come in. Twice, they had come to the front of the store because

SPOOKY SUDBURY

of the alert, only to find the shop empty. Frustrated by the disruptions, the girls pulled the doorbell off the wall.

Not long after, the girls were at the front of the shop where they would begin filling the shelves with fresh-baked treats. That's when they noticed the massive glass door, set inside a heavy stainless steel frame, open. There was a gap of about three inches between the door and the frame. No one was around, and the door was simply too heavy to move on its own.

"The girls couldn't understand how it could have opened," Cindy said. But Cindy knew exactly what happened — Suzy was just keeping her word.

"I started to tear up," she said. "I know it was her. Before she passed, she told me that if I see or hear something weird, that it's her. This was very comforting and reassuring for me and it still is to this day."

When an invisible force rubbed up against Cindy's arm, she knew again it was Suzy at work.

"There was nothing there," Cindy said. "I believe it was Suzy."

There is still a pair of shoes that once belonged to Suzy sitting in the shop. They rest right where she left them. Her old kitchen furniture now decorates the shop, and one of her handwritten inspirational notes is still on the chalkboard.

"Suzy always put positive phrases on that chalkboard," Cindy said. "One of my employees was going to clean it off one day recently … and something came over her not to erase it."

To this day, the message still reads "A good snapshot stops the moment from running away …" A fitting last phrase from Suzy.

Not only do her comforting words continue to drive Cindy to succeed, her dear friend's presence is never far away.

THE BELL MANSION

If there ever was a couple that Sudbury could call its own, it would undoubtedly be William and Katherine Bell. The enterprising young duo left a lasting legacy in Sudbury — their namesake is all over the city.

Perhaps the most concrete reminder of their lives spent in Sudbury is their former homestead, which is now home to the Art Gallery of Sudbury. The Bell Mansion was redone after it was entirely gutted by fire on December 3, 1955. The outer shell still remains the same.

The house, which qualifies as a mansion by just about every set of standards, was the result of a lifetime of hard work.

It was a few years before 1900 when the two arrived in Sudbury from Pembroke, Ontario. Soon after arriving, young William — a former lumberjack — became the manager of the Sable and Spanish River Boom and Slide Company. Within five years, he worked up the ranks, becoming vice-president and general manager of the Spanish River Lumber Company. It didn't take long before he merged into a partnership with the company's president William Benjamin Arnold, becoming half-in-charge of Arnold & Bell, a logging operation that operated along the North Shore.

It was the first of numerous entrepreneurial moves on Bell's part.

In 1924, he became the owner of the Spanish River Lumber Company and held on to the role of president until he sold to it in 1932. At the same time, his professional interests continued to grow. By 1920, he was president of Cochrane-Dunlop Hardware Company, and president and director of National Grocers Ltd.

Unsurprisingly, his business endeavours resulted in a prosperous life.

"The guy became a multi-millionaire at the time," recalls Gordon Drysdale. For years, Drysdale has been researching the Bells and has been heavily involved with efforts to restore their homestead. He plays an active part in the Friends of Belrock group.

Drysdale said to call William successful was not nearly enough.

The same year McLeod Motors, which we know now as Cambrian Ford, was selling Model T Fords for less than $500, William was driving a Packard Phaeton — the first new car in Sudbury — with a ticket price of $6,500.

It was hardly all work. Outside of his professional roles, William was a staunch supporter of the Conservative Party, a respected member of the United Church, serving as secretary and treasurer for St. Andrew's United Church, and a member of the Masonic Order. He was involved with the Sudbury Hockey Club and active in the formation of the Idylwylde Golf Club. He advocated for the creation of parks, donating the land we know as Memorial Park in downtown Sudbury, and of course, the 155 acres of green space surrounding Lake Ramsey, known as Sudbury's much loved Bell Park.

In 1942, his good works were honoured by the City of Sudbury, and his portrait, painted by C.A. McGrego, was hung

The Bell Mansion

in the City of Sudbury's Council Chambers. William was eighty-seven years old when he passed away in January 1945, due to complications from a leg injury.

Katherine outlived him by a number of years. She was ninety-two when she died, alone in the house.

"She left the house to the Memorial Hospital," Drysdale said. It served as a nurse's residence until fire destroyed the interior. The Nickel Lodge Masons bought it, but zoning complications saw it sit idle for nearly a decade. The doors and windows were boarded up, and the inside remained in shambles.

The building remained empty until 1966, when the property was purchased by the Centennial Committee of the Chamber of Commerce. In 1968, it was officially transferred to Laurentian University, who now leases the space to the art gallery.

"Although neither the Bell name nor much of the original interiors still grace this facility, we are grateful for the pioneering

This photograph of Bell Mansion was taken on August 21, 2011, at 1:30 a.m. by Steve Ripley, a Sudbury area spirit investigator.

SPOOKY SUDBURY

spirit and generosity of W.J. and Katherine Bell, which will always be associated with this site," the Art Gallery of Sudbury states on their website.

While the art gallery currently occupies the old mansion, many say Katherine has never left.

Her obituary said the community-minded woman would be "long remembered … for her generous nature and philanthropic works."

Much like William, Katherine was always on the go. She too was involved with St. Andrew's United Church, and played a big part in bringing the Victorian Order of Nurses to Sudbury. Katherine was also responsible for starting the Sudbury Horticultural Society. When she wasn't in the garden, she was near one of her beloved four-legged creatures. Katherine was known for her love of animals — so much so that she rarely ever rode in her husband's car. More often than not, she would get around by horse and buggy. She advocated for horses working in lumber camps, ensuring their fair and responsible treatment.

While she undoubtedly had a soft spot for animals, her caring nature didn't extend to other vulnerable groups — it has been said Katherine despised children.

There are rumours that during the early years, the sound of crying children could be heard coming from the gallery. Were these pre-recorded cries played for purpose of trying to keep the ghost of Katherine away?

During the summer of 2011, Steve Ripley, a curious Sudburian with a fascination for the Bell legacy, decided to explore the old mansion grounds to see what he could find. Curious by nature, Ripley likes to think there is a reasonable explanation for everything. He approached the property with an open mind, on the lookout for scientific proof of the possibility of spirit activity and

90

the afterlife. He brought along an audio recorder and a camera to see what he could find.

The night Ripley ventured to the John Street house was a quiet one. It had rained the night before, but the warm summer sun that sat high in the sky earlier had dried everything completely. "There was no wind at all," Ripley recalled. "It was dead silent."

His audio recorder didn't capture anything out of the ordinary, but his camera did. On two separate occasions, he photographed circular balls of light — almost comparable to bubbles floating in his camera's line of sight. The naked eye couldn't see anything, and when he took a second "control" photograph right after capturing the glowing orbs, nothing strange appeared.

Rational as he is, Ripley tried to come up with practical reasons for why the photos turned out the way they did.

"At first, I thought it was dust," he said. "But there was no dust in the air. It was something I couldn't explain. There was no logical reason for this to happen."

Was Katherine doing her rounds, checking on the grounds and gardens she once loved?

Ripley isn't the only one who has experienced strange things around the old Bell Mansion. Kimberly Fahner, a local poet and high school teacher, spent the early part of her career in the old building. Her encounter with Katherine is described here:

In 1997, I worked as communications officer for the Art Gallery of Sudbury. The gallery office at the time was located in the B.A. MacDonald House across the street from the rear of the Bell Rock Mansion, which housed the gallery itself. For most of my time at the art gallery, I worked regular hours, from 8:30 a.m.

until 4:30 p.m., in the office, but during the summer of that year, the director made the decision to staff the gallery space on certain week nights, to increase visitor attendance rates. It seemed a logical idea. I would come in later and work from noon until 8:00 p.m. I didn't think anything of it until I spoke to the museum guard, an older man who had worked there for a very long time. He shook his head when I told him of my schedule change. "You sure you want to do that?" When I pressed him, trying to figure out what he meant by the comment, he responded with "You might meet Mrs. Bell, is all." I laughed, thinking it was a joke.

Later that same week, though, another museum security guard, a young woman, chatted with me about my new schedule. "I've seen and heard things here," she told me, "like footsteps walking above me, in Gallery 3, while I'm at my station and I know that there's no one else in the building." As I listened, I chalked the occurrences up to the building settling or shifting, as old buildings do, and tried to put it out of my mind. After all, the following week I would have to be the only person in the building in the evenings, so I did not want to hear a story about mysterious ghostly footsteps. However, as the guard went on, her story only got stranger and my blood ran cold. She recounted a tale of how, at closing one night, she had to make her way down to the basement, check to see the bathrooms were empty, and then move up two flights of stairs to Galleries 2 and 3. Gallery 1 is on the main floor, as is the guard station. She had made her way upstairs and, after turning off the lights in Gallery 3, she walked back through Gallery 2 to return to the stairway. The guard had a sense that someone else was there and, as she was moved to go downstairs, she turned her head and saw the figure of a woman in Edwardian clothing walk across the floor through the doorway leading to Gallery 3. The figure was that of a solid person, not misty or ethereal. It

THE BELL MANSION

was Mrs. Bell. Needless to say, the guard booted it downstairs and locked the front door behind her.

My experience happened a week or two after speaking with both guards. It had been a relatively quiet day at work, but as the early evening set in, the atmosphere changed. It seemed charged somehow. I had finished my paperwork for the day's shift and so wandered into the gallery from the guard station, admiring the exhibit that was on display. I loved the way the lights cut through the gallery space and illuminated the artwork. Then, I wandered into the conservatory space. This quaint little room is the only original room that remained after the fire of 1955. It was painted white, with a meticulously tiled floor. There were a couple of plants left there to conjure up the past for visitors, and a little bench to perch on. I sat down, flipped through an exhibition guide, and enjoyed the silence. When I got nervous, I always just talked to Mrs. Bell. "Hey, I'd rather not see you, but I totally believe you're here … so you don't have to prove it to me, okay?" I thought I'd make a deal and avoid being terrified or startled.

Sometimes, when there weren't any visitors at all in the gallery, I would stand in the middle of Gallery 1 and just sing. I loved the acoustics. I know, it doesn't sound professional, but when you're faced with a bit of fear, an empty gallery, and rumours of ghosts, well, singing loudly seems a logical response to settle the nerves. I was singing an old traditional Irish tune. Suddenly, I heard a humming sound. It wasn't just a steady hum, but had the lyrical sounds and structure of a song. I paused in my singing, thinking maybe someone was passing on the driveway at the back of the building, so I rushed back into the conservatory and looked out the windows. Soon, the humming seemed to morph into something stronger, stringing itself through Gallery 1 and moving up the stairs. It was the sound of a woman's voice

SPOOKY SUDBURY

singing. It was soft, distant, but it was there. Mrs. Bell was singing, in response to my singing.

Now, when I think of it, I wonder how that could have happened. I've had odd ghostly encounters a few times in my life. They're all unique to a place, but I always feel better if I speak to them. If I recognize them as having been people, just like me, then they're less scary and pretty interesting. To commemorate my encounter with Mrs. Bell's singing ghost, I wrote a poem, *Ghost of a Chance*, which was published in my second book of poems. I want to remember that evening and the duet I shared with Mrs. Bell.

(The poem is from the book titled *Braille on Water*, published by Penumbra Press in 2001.)

Ghost of a Chance

alone,
one night,
shadowed by moon
and hoping
to catch
even just
a glimpse
of you.

wind outside,
quiet inside,
while something
stirs within skin.

THE BELL MANSION

fetal heartbeat
of spirit
drumming a
fierce raindance
on the roof above me.

thinking that maybe
you'll come inside,
in weather such as this.

when the sky weeps
and fades to the
colour of oysters
on a bright wet day.

Who could blame Katherine for continuing to live at the mansion? After all, it has always been her home.

I'll Be Back

Curiosity toward the unknown seems to be genetic. Sally Matwichuk was certain her mom was still around, even after she passed away. Sally would even go as far as telling her kids that her mom was never far; still playing jokes and watching over the family.

Before Sally passed away, she too assured her family she would never be far.

"She always said she'd be back," her son Sean Barrette said. "Mom didn't bullshit anyone and was always good for her word — you knew where you stood. So, if she said she was coming back, she was coming back."

And that's exactly what she did. The fiercely intelligent, passionate woman with the exceptional sense of humour died, surrounded by family, on November 13, 2003, in Kapuskasing. She was fifty-three. Sean had driven north to be with her in her final hours, while his wife Lara Newell-Barrette stayed home to make some arrangements.

After he said his goodbyes and took some time to let the reality set in, he phoned home to tell his wife.

When she got on the phone, Sean said, "Mom is gone."

"I know," Lara replied.

Sean instantly wondered if someone already phoned her. It wasn't the phone that alerted her though — turns out Sally had decided to surprise Lara with a visit. A half hour or so before, around the time Sally took her last breath, the front doors of the Barrette household swung open simultaneously.

Despite the declining weather, Laura knew it was impossible for the doors to both open at the same time. No gust of wind could have been responsible for it because one front door opens outward and the other opens inward. To top it off, Lara was certain she locked both doors not long before.

"In thirteen years in our house it hadn't happened before, or since," Sean said.

"You'll have a hard time convincing me that she didn't come to say goodbye to Lara, and prove that she had been right all along and was never going to be too far away. And she'd have thought making such a grand entrance by throwing those two locked doors open was hilarious."

Lara said the experience was so real that it's impossible to even consider it "unexplainable."

"I guess I feel comforted and kind of like 'wow … that was pretty cool,' but I don't really see it as being scary or even that unusual," she said. In fact, it was "peaceful" to know Sally had come by for a last visit.

Still, she isn't far. Lara said "without a doubt" that Sally is still around.

"I don't really consider things like this 'out of the ordinary,' but there are many times when I get a very strong sense that Sally, or her energy at least, is around us," Lara said. "It's hard to explain — it's just a knowing."

When Lara was pregnant with her and Sean's first child, Sally

SPOOKY SUDBURY

made sure to bring her some motherly wisdom. Lara was hospitalized with a fairly serious birth condition called complete placenta previa.

"One night, I had a 'visit' from Sally," she said. "It was the middle of the night, and I woke up to the sensation of someone sitting on the end of my bed. For a brief second, I saw her sitting there — not in a solid form so much — more like a hazy figure. She smiled and in that moment, I knew that everything would be okay with the baby."

After that, even during the most intense times, Lara was able to stay calm.

"The nurses would have to come rushing in to put monitors on and do their job, they would often make comments about how calm I was and that most people in my situation would not be handling it so well," she said. "I never told anyone except my husband and a few immediate family members about the 'visit,' but that was the reason why I was so calm. I just knew that everything was going to be okay. In the end, it was."

Reassuring news, coming from one mama to another. It's nice to know it will be okay.

ALONG THE NORTH SHORE

"Downbound Superior,
Along the North Shore,
I'm heading to Goderich,
I've been there before,
But I'm packing my bags getting off in the Soo,
Going home to see Mommy, Stacey, Julie and you."
— Lori Holmes-McIntyre

When the wind blows, Cory Holmes-McIntyre can hear old sailor songs. He was young, only about two years old, when he stopped his mother in her tracks by singing along with her.

Lori Holmes-McIntyre was mindlessly folding laundry one day in her son's bedroom, humming and singing her dad's old songs. Harvey Holmes was a sailor before he moved his family to Elliot Lake. When they arrived in the Northern community, he traded his ship for a hard hat, taking a job in the mine. Lori only had the first thirteen years of her life to get to know him, before he passed away. In those years, however, she distinctly remembers listening to him sing.

"He'd always sing that song to us," she recalled.

Lori had gotten through the first line of the song before Cory chimed in.

"Downbound Superior," she sang.

"Along the Norf Shore," he sang back, in traditional child-speak.

"I looked at him and asked him what he said, and he said it again; 'Along the Norf Shore.' I asked him how he knew that song, and he said he hears it singing when the wind blows."

Lori said there's no way Cory could have heard the song from anyone but her, and she doesn't recall ever teaching her young son the words. She was initially thrown off by her son's statement, but she smiled once the initial shock wore off. It bothered her that her dad had never got to meet her kids.

"I wasn't scared by it, and I didn't want to scare him," she said. "It was comforting to know my dad was around, and that he could see the kids. It still saddens me that my boys didn't get to have him in their day-to-day life."

This wasn't the only time Lori and her sisters were shocked by her father's unexplainable presence. Her younger sister, who lives in Sault Ste. Marie, was chatting to her young son when he out of the blue asked "Where is Grandpa Harvey?"

Her sister warmly told the three-year-old that "he's up in heaven," as she had many times before.

The youngster knew otherwise, though.

"No he's not," he said, looking past his mom. "He's right there, smoking a pipe."

Lori's sister didn't see anything when she turned around, but it was true Harvey was often seen with a pipe in his mouth.

That gave Lori an extra bit of reassurance that Harvey was, in fact, watching her boys grow up.

CAPREOL RED AND THE
CAPREOL HIGH CUSTODIAN

S mall towns are a breeding ground for stories and tall tales. Perhaps it is because they are also a breeding ground for characters. The town of Capreol is, of course, no exception to this fine rule.

Capreol Red, a man who worked as a railroad copy back in the days of steam power, was also no exception and one of that town's more notorious characters. Known — and feared — up and down the line, he was considered to be a hard man during hard times. Stories about Red continue to be shared to this day, and, in the telling, they continue to grow and to stretch, the way that stories in a small town have that special way of becoming something larger with each new telling.

When Capreol author Matthew Del Papa started listening to the tall tales of local railroad men, he was so swept up in the stories that he forgot the common understanding that he should have taken everything a railroader says with a grain of salt.

"Unfortunately, I forgot this bit of local wisdom," Del Papa says. "So while the title story of my book *The Legend of Capreol*

Red: And Other Stories From a Railroad Town was based on what I thought was fact … only later did I learn the truth."

Del Papa learned that the man, Capreol Red, did not in fact die under strange circumstances. That particular twist — probably wishful thinking on somebody's part — was dreamt up by a railroader. By then it was too late, Del Papa was hooked and had pursued a need to write the story of Red's death.

And that's the thing about stories — if they're well told it doesn't matter whether they are true or not. But, while Matthew Del Papa's book is fiction based on tall tales, the following story, which he uncovered in the winter of 2013, has an eerie ring of truth, and the echoes of the tale remind us of the spooky tales that we often overheard in the playground of our school yards.

The Capreol High Custodian
By Matthew Del Papa

High school is a scary place. In fact, most people can't wait to get out. But that's not the case at Capreol High. There someone lingers … or rather the spirit of someone. That's right, Capreol High School is haunted. Though the school closed in the late 1990s, its empty halls still echo with the sound of booted feet and the jingling of keys. According to former students and faculty, unexplained sounds were once common and, some say, still are.

The school had many dedicated employees over the years — one, the custodian, is still there despite being long dead.

He's never been seen. Only heard. So how do they know it's the custodian? The keys. The man never went anywhere without his ring of keys. They hung off his belt and rattled with every step. Students and faculty all knew the sound. They'd hear it during class as he moved past sweeping the halls or during after-school

CAPREOL RED AND THE CAPREOL HIGH CUSTODIAN

activities as he emptied the trash cans. The school couldn't operate if it wasn't for the custodian and his keys — every day he'd unlock the doors and every evening he'd lock them back up.

A big man, the custodian took pride in his work and his school ... and he always thought of it as *his* school. His dedication knew no limit. Often he'd be at work on the weekend, polishing the floors, washing the windows, or scraping gum out from under desks. Every step accompanied by the sound of rattling keys.

The day of his funeral his widow hung those keys in their usual spot beside the front door. She left to attend the service and when she returned they were gone. Never to be seen again.

Only heard.

Details vary, but rumours of the Capreol High Ghost persist. Even now, more than a decade after the school's closing, some refuse to stay in the building alone, and to this day, people report strange noises in the former high school, now the Capreol Millennium Resource Centre. Most believe that the spirit is harmless, the custodian merely going about his routine — after death as he had in life — with his keys jingling with every disembodied step.

THE ENTITY IN HALLOWEEN HOUSE

Halloween is a big deal for Rose Anne Cardinal and her fiancé Adam Kehoe. Since moving into their Flour Mill area home in 2010, the young couple have been adding decorations, intentionally making it more and more eerie — at least for one night a year. Every October, they create a spooky scene complete with battered planks, skeletons, and a ghostly graveyard. There's a fog machine and splattered "blood" too, just for extra effect.

As far as Kehoe is concerned, Halloween is the highlight of the year. He loves everything about the season: the darkness, the sound effects, and the traditional spookiness of the occasion.

"Halloween is better than Christmas," he said.

And it's only just beginning.

"I want to be known as 'the house we have to go to,'" Kehoe said. "I think people like it."

While some enjoy the thrill, others opt to stay away.

"The kids were scared last year to come to our door," Cardinal said.

THE ENTITY IN HALLOWEEN HOUSE

Maybe it is simply the man-made setup that makes the old two-storey home next to the train tracks on Melvin Street so dreadful. Or maybe there's more to it.

Both Cardinal and Kehoe try to refrain from talking about "the entity" that shares their home. By not acknowledging it, they believe they can happily co-exist, with only a few minor hiccups. Like the time both of them heard the sound of what they describe as "old feet" creeping up to their bedroom.

It was March 2010. While lying in bed, the sound of slippers dragging across the floor had caught Kehoe's attention. He sat up and froze, peering out into the hallway.

"I always have this fear of having a door open, and being able to see out that door," Kehoe said. Staring at the empty hallway while the sound became clearer and clearer did nothing to calm his nerves.

By the time the sound was halfway up the stairs, Cardinal was wide awake too.

"I thought there was somebody in our house," she said.

Crippled with fear, the two held their breath as they waited.

"I was waiting for someone to appear in the doorway," Kehoe said. No visible figure appeared, but the sound didn't go away.

In a state of panic, Kehoe decided to jump into action. As he leaped out of bed, he didn't bother to cover his naked body. Instead, he latched on to the nearest thing he could find — he pulled a samurai sword off the wall.

He flicked on every light switch as he bounded toward the hallway. Once every light in the house had been turned on, it was clear that Cardinal and Kehoe were alone.

The result was a poor night's sleep, but nothing else was out of order.

"Life carried on," Kehoe said.

Both Cardinal and Kehoe try to refrain from talking about "the entity" that they share their home with. By not acknowledging it, they believe they can happily co-exist.

It wasn't until that summer that they were reminded of their shared residence. By this time, the couple's Jack Russell Terrier, Ozzy, had made a habit of playing with his toys upstairs. Anytime the small dog had a toy, he'd bring it to the second storey of the home and chew and comp away. Both Cardinal and Kehoe had become accustomed to the sound of balls rolling across the floor and the little dog chasing after them. They were standing downstairs, and initially didn't think much of the noises coming from above.

"It sounded like a softball," Kehoe said. "They have that distinct sound when you drop them. We heard it fall from the bed and you could hear it hit the floor."

THE ENTITY IN HALLOWEEN HOUSE

That was until the dog caught their eye from a window. He had been outside the entire time, playing with the very ball they had both heard crash onto the floor above them. When they went upstairs to investigate, they were greeted by empty space.

"There was nothing on the floor in any room," Kehoe said.

The family pets have experienced other strange happenings. One on occasion, Kehoe was walking up the stairs while their German shepherd, Diesel, stood at the top, looking down.

"He didn't do anything," Kehoe said. "He just stood there. Then he got defensive."

As Kehoe looked quizzically at the dog, he realized Diesel wasn't even looking at him.

"He wasn't looking at me," he said. "He was looking past me, growling a deep growl. He knew there was something there." Instantly spooked by the dog's strong reaction, Kehoe hurried to the top of the stairs and didn't look back.

There have been countless other times when both Ozzy and Diesel seem distracted by an invisible being — one that mesmerizes them.

"You just know there's something here," Kehoe said. Rumors say a train once derailed from the tracks which rest right along their property line. Whether it's true or not, it's a story the couple likes to believe.

While the eerie activity has been regular, it hasn't been constant. It hasn't been enough to drive out the young couple either.

"I try not to think about it," Cardinal said. It seems that when they consciously feed into the energy, it becomes more active. Moments before they let me into their house to chat about the odd things that happen, a Christmas decoration fell off their tree and shattered into pieces on the ground.

It's a happier existence when both the living residents and the non-living choose to give each other their own space.

THE ENERGIES PRESENT

Anne Boulton spent her childhood growing up among the black rocks of Copper Cliff. The town was old when she lived there — her first home, a former bakery, had already been standing a century when she and her family moved in. In the old wooden bakery, which still stands today, Anne had a big room she shared with her brother. There were no hallways on the top floor, so in order to get to the spacious upper-level bedroom, Anne and her brother had to walk through her sister's room.

This is where Anne's experiences with the paranormal began. It would be the first of many places she would encounter the unexplained.

Even now, two decades later, Anne vividly recalls a night when she called her mom to tuck her in. She was lying in bed, facing the wall as she heard footsteps walking through the adjoining room and into hers. Comfortable and content, Anne listened as what she thought was her mother sat down on the bed next to her.

"The bed sunk down," Anne recalled. "I felt myself being tucked in. Then, I turned around and no one was there."

THE ENERGIES PRESENT

A little spooked by what had happened, Anne didn't know how to respond. She tried everything she could to justify the situation; Maybe she was she just being young and imaginative. Maybe she was drifting in and out of sleep.

Even if she did tell someone, she wondered what they could do or say to resolve the incident.

She kept the story of the invisible presence to herself, but never forgot the out-of-the-ordinary experience. When news came up that her family would be moving to a house located just one block away, Anne wondered if the bizarre occurrences would continue.

"Would they follow me?" she wondered.

Shortly after moving into the big, old boarding house, odd things began happening again. This time, however, they didn't feel quite so benevolent.

"The house just felt spooky," Anne recalled. "I felt like I was always complaining to my parents (about strange things) at this point."

One of the first occurrences she remembers was arriving home from school one day to an empty house. Anne walked into the kitchen just in time to watch a glass literally fly off the middle of the counter before smashing into pieces on the floor. She still gets goosebumps now when she recalls the incident.

On another occasion, Annie — by then a teenager — was sitting in the cellar in the dark, far away from the family, arguing with her then-boyfriend on the phone.

At the time, "the anger in the conversation surpassed any fears" about being in the already creepy basement, she said.

However, somewhere between heated words, an eerie aura quickly became too obvious to ignore. Her conversation was halted when she became aware of a low, slow whistling sound coming from the cement below her feet. She tried to ignore it for the sake

SPOOKY SUDBURY

of carrying on the conversation, but couldn't bring herself to. The phone call and the obvious noise ended when she hurried upstairs.

"They kept going until I left for the main floor," Anne said.

After experiencing enough oddities on her own, Anne was almost relieved when her friends began noticing strange things happening. It meant, at the very least, she wasn't making up the strange events. Anne and her friend Cheryl were on their way home from school when they were going to what they thought was Anne's empty house.

"Cheryl said, 'Is someone here? I thought I could see someone in the basement,' she asked as she looked down the stairs leading to the lower level."

Knowing the house was empty, Anne went to prove it.

"Come out, come out, wherever you are," she called through the empty house. Just as soon as the said the words, the sound of hurried footsteps filled the house. Both Anne and Cheryl heard what sounded like a group of people running carelessly through the house, crashing and banging into walls and falling onto the floor.

"There was this big noise with no bodies," Anne said.

Not wanting to know what could possibly be making the horrendous sound, the girls left. They didn't even bother closing the fridge door before making their escape. She didn't dare go back into the house until the rest of the family was home.

While Anne has left the outlying community of Copper Cliff to make a home for herself in Sudbury, she has continued to keep an open mind in the energies present in the places she has lived in and visited. The old cozy home she currently shares with her nine-year-old son and partner has never caused her any concern.

A few odd and unexplainable things have taken place since she moved in three years ago, but none of them have ever left her spooked.

The Energies Present

"We have good energy," she said. "If there is something here, it's accepting."

However, when her son complains about weird noises and refuses to go upstairs alone, Anne knows well enough to give him the benefit of the doubt.

THE HOSPITAL

When the Sisters of St. Joseph of Sault Ste Marie sold St. Joseph's to a private developer, a few fortunate Sudburians had the chance to take one last walk through it, documenting the final days of the hospital. Although much had already been taken out, a few pieces of equipment had been left behind. Tom Rogers (not his real name) was part of a small group that was privileged to walk the eerie deserted hallways of the facility that saw so many people take their first breath, and so many take their last.

He and a local photographer went back to the empty building multiple times during April 2010. Tom said in the weeks shortly after it had closed, the entire building "looked like it was humming with energy," even from the outside. When he arrived the first time, security guards confirmed Tom's hunches.

"There's very strange energy in this place," guards told him.

Well aware of what he was getting into, Tom didn't want to miss the opportunity to explore the building. Upon entering, the first thing that caught his attention was the walls.

"It's like a going away card," Tom said. "People had written all over the walls. Everybody signed it." Their messages varied

The Hospital

— some had recounted tales of their days working in the hospital, others simply said farewell, and some wrote what appeared to be inside jokes. The etchings on the wall only added to the spooky aura around the building, Tom said.

On one of his first visits, he went in the early evening. Tom had made it well into the building before he encountered his first strange experience. He was exploring the top floor of the south wing, some six floors high, when a breeze fluttered over his head. All the windows were closed, and Tom knew full well he was alone.

"I was the only one in the hospital at the time," he said. Recalling the experience, he couldn't help but shudder. Not wanting to jump to conclusions, Tom surveyed his surroundings. He looked around, but no possible explanation for a breeze existed.

While he was rattled after the unexplainable breeze, Tom knew he wanted to see more. He returned several times after that.

On one occasion, he was in the former emergency room waiting area, snapping photos of piles of discarded equipment. By this time, all the information and data storage devices had been moved into storage, and anything electronic had been unplugged. Still, a sign indicating which patient was being served was still aglow. Tom took several photos of it over his visits to the facility. In April, the sign read "Now serving number eighty-six." By the end of June, the staff was ready to see patient ninety-one.

"All there was in emerg was a computer and a desk," Tom said. "There's no way the sign would have been connected to anything."

On another visit, Tom's journey took him to the sub-basement. Only one elevator in the building went down to that level.

"It was cold — I could almost see my breath," he recalled. As he wandered about, he noted the honeycomb-patterned flooring.

Spooky Sudbury

He didn't get much farther than fifteen steps from the elevator when a sound stopped him. There was no doubt about what he heard.

"No one is going to believe this one," he said. But what he heard was loud and clear.

"I heard this little girl giggling," he said. "She dropped a bag of alleys, and kept giggling harder." He was close enough to the elevator to make an escape before he heard what she did next.

During his subsequent visits to the hospital, Tom said the atmosphere had changed significantly. As the spring weather warmed into summer, he said he couldn't spend more than an hour and a half inside the facility before "needing" to get out.

"It was hard to breathe almost, it (the air) was so heavy," Tom said. "The longer that place sits, the spookier it gets."

Tom believes that the site of the old hospital should be left alone.

"Everybody went there — they were born there and they died there," he said. "Energy doesn't leave. It's sacred ground."

MORGAN ROAD

When Ellen Roy (not her real name) first moved onto Morgan Road with her now-ex-husband Greg, she was happy as could be. The two lived in the mobile home with the extension and full basement for about nine years, beginning in 1995.

Ellen loved having a bit of acreage and a small barn for her horses right outside her home, in her backyard.

The place they called home was nothing but warm until the couple welcomed their first child. As soon as her son Todd was born, Ellen couldn't shake "this odd feeling."

"Some may call it paranoia, but it was very, very real," she said. The young mom would forever watch Todd, to make sure he was breathing. A fear of Sudden Infant Death Syndrome (SIDS) had her worried sick.

Once Ellen began noticing the "feeling of doom," it became harder and harder to ignore. The more energy she fed to it, the more evident it became. One day, she was home alone when the top of a wine bottle mysteriously popped off, gushing wine everywhere.

"I would always make up excuses like the bottle was on its side and got warm and somehow that caused a chemical reaction with the wine and somehow, it popped off," she said. But she was the first to know it was an excuse. "Other odd things would happen but it wasn't so much that odd things would happen so much as this really bad feeling I had."

While the entire house became more and more eerie, Ellen was most concerned about the heavy feeling in the corner of the master bedroom. Both Todd and the daughter who followed a few years later spent the first year of their life in a cradle in that corner.

"There is just bad energy there and it is under the front steps, which is off the master bedroom," Ellen said.

The feeling wasn't one she shared readily — Ellen knew Greg "was a total controlling freak," and would make fun of her for worrying over nothing. Knowing her "gut has always been right,"

Once Ellen began noticing the "feeling of doom," it became harder and harder to ignore.

Morgan Road

she had to do something though. Ellen eventually did confide in a good friend and neighbor — a woman who soon after brought over a bottle of holy water and a protective prayer for Ellen to say to her children.

It worked, as Ellen and her two children moved out of the house in 2004 unharmed. The people who moved in next, however, weren't quite so lucky.

Years after the place had sold Ellen heard some terribly haunting news about the sweet young couple who bought the farm after she moved out. Shortly after they had their first child, the family that called 1716 Morgan Road home fell victim to her biggest fear; their baby passed away from SIDS.

"SIDS was my fear and I seemed to stave that off but someone else's baby died. Coincidence?"

After the baby died, it's said the young mom never returned to the house. After they sold the farm, the new owners who purchased the property lost the barn to a fire.

Since moving away, Ellen no longer experiences the negative energy that she felt so strongly in the house on Morgan Road.

THE CHELMSFORD GHOST

As the creator of the website ParaNorthern.ca, Mitch Ross is certainly curious about the unexplained. However, the Sudbury-based marketing specialist has a hard time believing anything he can't explain — that's why he never claims to have seen a ghost.

"I saw it several times over several years," he said. "What 'it' was, I don't know."

The sight Mitch is referring to is an adult-sized, human-shaped figure made of what looked like thousands of little lights.

"It looked sort of like a glow," he said.

The first time he encountered the apparition, Mitch was seven years old. His open bedroom doorway looked out to the hallway where he could see part way around the corner into the kitchen, and at the opposite end of the hall, the bathroom. It was near the beginning of October, the first fall after his parents had moved into the Chelmsford house.

"The first time, I thought my dad pulled some trick on us," he said. However, when a scared young Mitch went to tell his

THE CHELMSFORD GHOST

parents about the strange glowing aura, they laughed it off as an overactive imagination.

"I got told 'don't be ridiculous, and go back to bed,'" Mitch recalled.

It was a task easier said than done.

"It's hard to sleep when the wheels are spinning," he said.

After making it through the night, Mitch was ready for a solid rest the following evening. However, like clockwork, the glow walked from the kitchen, past his open bedroom door once again, and disappeared into the bathroom.

"When it happened again, I was really scared," Mitch said. For three nights in a row, the glow moved past his bedroom door, while a terrified young Mitch looked on.

On the third night, the glow walked into the bathroom and disappeared for good — or so Mitch thought. It wasn't until a year later that Mitch was revisited by the entity. When October rolled around again, the youngster found himself once again watching the glowing apparition float by his door. The first night it happened, he was alone in the house.

"It scared the living hell out of me," he said.

After that, he slept with the door closed. For five years, however, the glow would sneak up on him at least once at the beginning of the month.

"Since then, I've never seen anything that accurately described what I saw," he said. After the initial shock of seeing the light orb left him, Mitch said he never felt like it was there to cause harm.

"It always felt like something that had been left behind," he said.

It wasn't until years later, long after Mitch had relocated his bedroom to the basement, that he learned a chilling truth about his family home. He was about seventeen years old when the previous home owners returned for a final goodbye.

Spooky Sudbury

"The people who owned the house before us stopped to visit the place because they were moving down south," he said. "They were telling us the reason they sold the house was because they had a son who died in his crib."

The little boy passed away at the beginning of October, when he was about a year-and-a-half old. His crib had been placed in the corner of Mitch's room. The family left a little over a year after they lost him.

After hearing the family recount their story, Mitch began making sense of the strange things he'd seen every fall during his childhood. He also believed the spirit of the baby was responsible for the cold energy in the corner of his bedroom.

When he lived in the upstairs room, he could never have his bed in the place the crib was. It was always far too cold to sleep in, despite being in the middle of the house.

Mitch was a young adult when circumstances led him back to the Chelmsford home. This time, he brought along a friend, who occupied the upstairs bedroom he had as a child, while Mitch stayed in his old basement room. His friend brought along a pet hamster, who lived happily in a cage on a dresser. When Mitch's mom needed the dresser, his friend simply moved the cage to the shelf in the corner.

Within days, the otherwise healthy animal was huddled up in a ball, frozen in the corner.

"We spent sixty-five dollars at the vet for a two dollar hamster to find out it was hibernating and not going to wake up," Mitch said. Thinking it might have just been chance, his friend bought another pet hamster. It too lived happily in the bedroom, until the cat caught sight of it. In order to prevent the mischievous feline from opening the cage, his friend once again moved the hamster to the corner. Within days, it too curled up into hibernation and passed away. When the third hamster passed

THE CHELMSFORD GHOST

away under the same conditions, it was clear there was something off about the space. In the span of two months, the cold spot in the corner zapped the life from three hamsters.

Mitch is certain the life lost in the corner has something to do with it.

THE NICKEL MINER'S GHOST

It was a fresh new century when, in newlywed bliss, Amanda, her husband, their daughter, and a red Doberman moved into the beautiful old house they had purchased in an established Sudbury neighbourhood. The gorgeous two-storey home had character and charm, but it also held a little something else that wouldn't fully reveal itself until a couple of years later, when their son arrived.

And though their very first night in the new home was a disturbing night to remember, the chills that later greeted them were never frightening, never threatening; they were merely eerie.

"Our first night at the house was a horror!" Amanda says with a bit of a grin.

They were exhausted from the day of moving, and the beautiful spa bath upstairs that had so attracted Amanda when they had been considering the home called to her like a siren beckoning a sailor on the open seas.

Amanda started the tub, filled it up, and then went downstairs to get a nice glass of wine to drink while relaxing in the tub. It wasn't until she was heading back upstairs that she heard

The Nickel Miner's Ghost

what sounded like rain inside the house. She ran back down to the kitchen to see water pouring from the pot lights in the kitchen ceiling.

As the water showered down, running everywhere and flooding the kitchen floor, Amanda screamed for her husband. Hot water was pouring everywhere as the two scrambled around the home trying to figure out how to stop the water from flooding — but the tub hadn't been overfilled — it was draining on its own.

The floors in the kitchen, dining room, and the hallways, all hardwood flooring, started buckling and were completely ruined. They had to be replaced. The renovation crew they hired explained that there was a crack in the tube that sucked the water from the tub and through the spa jets, which was the source of the leak.

The next strange thing that happened, before the events began to occur regularly, involved their eight-year-old daughter, who occasionally was overheard speaking to her imaginary friend. Having an imaginary friend is not an uncommon thing with children; although Amanda's daughter mentioned later that her friend was the nice man who had once lived in the home.

Amanda had heard the tragic tale of the miner who had been the previous homeowner. She and her husband had purchased the home from the miner's wife. She had very briefly explained that she was selling the house after the tragic mining accident that had suddenly taken her husband from her, not just because the home was too large for her, but that there were too many memories of her beloved in the home; memories that, though tender, still haunted her. So, sadly, she moved on.

The miner's mother lived next door and mostly kept to herself the first few years, nodding politely and greeting them with the occasional "good morning," or "good afternoon," or whatever seasonal greeting was appropriate.

Amanda had heard the tragic tale of the miner who had been the previous home owner.

Amanda had always felt bad for the woman, knowing, as every parent does, that one of the worst things that can happen to a parent is to lose their child.

Regular eerie events only began to occur once their baby boy arrived home, a couple of years after having moved into the house.

Amanda and her husband occasionally felt cold spots in their son's bedroom — sudden and localized plummets in temperature. Sometimes, the baby monitor would go on for no reason at all and the door to his room would close all by itself.

The times when, in the middle of the night, their son would wake up screaming, were quite terrifying to Amanda and her

husband, particularly when the child could not be easily con-
soled until he was removed from the room. "I had never heard a
baby scream like that before," Amanda said.

Their docile and family friendly Doberman, who regularly
slept in the bed with Amanda and her husband, occasionally
refused to go upstairs. It would pause on the middle landing
area of the stairs and refused to take another step forward, just
stand there, shackles up, shaking, and barking as if something or
someone was there.

Over the first few years, while their conversations with the
quiet old woman next door rarely went beyond quick mentions
of the weather or the latest news, on one occasion, the elderly
woman asked if Amanda's husband smoked.

"Why do you ask?" Amanda said.

"Sometimes," the woman sad in a quiet voice "I see a man
standing outside on your front steps, smoking at night."

The woman explained that every so often, late at night when
she was looking out her window, the one that gave her a clear
view of her son's old home, she would notice a man standing on
the front step and smoking, very much like her son used to do.
She didn't say anything about it for a long time, but curiosity got
the better of her and she decided to ask Amanda.

"Neither of us smokes," Amanda told her.

"It looks just like my son," the woman sad, with a sad, muted
smile on her face.

And though goosebumps pimpled up on Amanda's arm, it
also gave her a sentimental feeling. Thoughts that the man's spirit
might still be in the home left her with a sense of warmth. Yes,
their dog and their son seemed to be able to sense this presence
more clearly than anyone else, but, after their son's crying incidents ceased, nobody in the family ever felt unsafe or anything
but comforted in the home.

SPOOKY SUDBURY

Instead, Amanda and her family lived there for several more years in peace and comfort before moving out. And the whole time they were aware of the ethereal resident living with them; the figure whose occasional appearance, standing quietly on the front step smoking like he had done for years before he was taken from the world, seemed to bring a small sense of comfort and peace to the kind, quiet old woman next door who had lost her only son.

Scary Sudbury Skies:
UFOs, Flying Saucers, and Other Objects in the Sky

In 1975 multiple independent eyewitness civilian and police reports combined with radar tracking at Falconbridge led to a squadron of U.S. Air National Guard F-106 Interceptors sent to inspect Sudbury area skies

WE ARE NOT ALONE

Throughout the history of mankind, strange objects have been reported in the skies. Of course, over time, various cultures and societies have interpreted the bright lights or unexplainable objects seen in the day and night skies relative to the common belief of their time.

One of the earliest reports of an Unidentified Flying Object (UFO) comes from an ancient Indian text dating back to 500 B.C. In the *Samarangana-Sartadhara*, an encyclopedia work on classical Indian architecture, there is a passage that describes odd machines called vimanas, which fly and are controlled by pilots. Similar machines are referenced in Sanskrit (the classical language of India and Hinduism) in the texts *Mahabharata* and *Ramayana*, where the descriptions suggest these are military machines designed to "carry death."[1]

It wasn't until about 1947 that the term "flying saucer" was first used in connection with the increase in reports of flying discs, ghost rockets, and airships.[2] On a clear day on the 24th of June, 1947, Kenneth Arnold, an American aviator and business-man, was flying east over the Cascade Mountains in Washington

SPOOKY SUDBURY

state when he saw a tremendous flash. Arnold was immediately worried that he was about to crash into another aircraft; what he suspected was the reflection of the sun off a nearby plane, but there was nothing else visible other than a Douglas DC-4 airplane.[3]

Arnold then spied another flash to his left and spotted a formation of nine very bright objects flying extremely close to the mountain tops and at "tremendous speed." Arnold estimated that the objects were flying at over seventeen hundred miles per hour. This was substantial because it wasn't until later in 1947 that the sound barrier speed of seven hundred and fifty miles per hour was first shattered:[4]

> They didn't fly like any aircraft I had seen before … they flew in a definite formation, but erratically … their flight was like speed boats on rough water or similar to the tail of a Chinese kite that I once saw blowing in the wind … they fluttered and sailed, tipping their wings alternatively and emitting those very bright, blue-white flashes from their surfaces. At the time I did not get the impression that these flashes were emitted by them but rather that it was the sun's reflection from the extremely highly polished surfaces of their wings.[5]

The story was relayed by Arnold to a local newspaperman, and in that original article, Arnold explained that the craft flew like a stone being skipped across the water. Newspaperman Bill Becquette, of the *East Oregonian*, translated this phrase into "flying saucer," which seems to have helped propel the use of that term.[6]

A few years later, as part of Project Blue Book, a U.S. Air Force investigation on the phenomenon, a new term was devised to describe the occurrences. The air force desired a less emotive

WE ARE NOT ALONE

or descriptive term than saucer or disc, particularly since it made people think about the terms used in popular Hollywood B movies. Chief investigator, Captain Edward J. Ruppelt insisted on the use of "unidentified flying object." That term not only removed the description of the potential shape, but also did not imply the source or cause of the witnessed objects.[7]

In much of popular culture, the term UFO is commonly associated with "alien spacecraft" based upon decades of media speculation on the Extraterrestrial Hypothesis (ETH) — that the only plausible explanation for the phenomenon is related to alien technology rather than other reasons.[8]

To skeptics, UFOs are merely some sort of natural meteorological or geological phenomenon that has been misinterpreted by the witness; or perhaps they are simply a hallucination or blatant error in perception. The skeptics, however, are far outnumbered by the ufologists (people who are so interested in the subject that they have created numerous books, websites, and groups dedicated to the study and collection of reported cases).[9]

One such resource, championed by Michel Deschamps, called the Northern Ontario UFO Research & Study (NOUFORS) is dedicated to eyewitnesses, both past and present, and contains a plethora of documented cases of UFO sightings.

In an August 6, 1999, article in the *Northern Life*, Michel Deschamps, a long-time UFO watcher, believes that Sudbury is a veritable hotspot for otherworldly visitors.

"I think they're keeping a steady eye on the mining activity here." Deschamp says in the article written by Michael Whitehouse. Deschamps says that it is the consensus of Internet watchers that alien interest in Sudbury is both long-standing and based on our mining history.[10] Perhaps there is something in the high frequency of nickel deposits in our region that is attracting these visitors.

Spooky Sudbury

One of the earliest reports of a UFO in Sudbury came shortly after Kenneth Arnold's famous 1947 encounter. Just a few months later, as UFO sightings were beginning to grow in popular culture, in September of 1947, grade seven student Jack Trainor reported seeing a "large round object flying in a northerly direction at terrific speed." Trainor went on to describe the object as wobbling a bit as it went, not flying very high, and that it did not emit any smoke or vapour trail.[11]

In December of that same year, a group of at least twenty people witnessed a rocket-like object in the sky,[12] and in March 1948, two different truck drivers reported a mysterious flaming object in the sky. Joe Caruso, a transport truck driver, was making a delivery in Warren when he watched a jet-like object in the sky for as long as ten minutes before it shot off into the horizon and disappeared. Frank Forth, another truck driver who was perhaps three hundred metres behind Caruso, saw the same thing. They both stopped their trucks for fear that the streaking object might strike them. They described the object as approximately eighty feet long and oval-shaped with orange coloured sparks about twenty feet long shooting from the rear. The object made a U-turn and then followed alongside them at approximately forty kilometres per hour about one hundred and fifty feet to the right hand side of the road, before a freight train came into view; that was when the object suddenly gained speed and disappeared into the northern sky. The newspaper report from March 20, 1948, also mentions similar events reported within a two-week period in Moose Factory, James Bay, and in Cochrane.[13]

This, of course, was just the beginning, as hundreds of cases of UFO sightings have been reported in the Sudbury region since then. This section of the book takes a bit of a closer look at just some of those sightings.

THE 1950S: THE RACE TO (AND FROM) SPACE

In the post-war era, North America was still recovering from World War II and its citizens prayed for a period of peace. However, new political conflicts soon arose, such as the Cold War, the Korean War, and the Vietnam War. Rock and roll emerged as the popular music of choice for teens, with artists such as Chuck Berry, Bobby Darin, and Elvis Presley emerging into a culture that was also enjoying the rise of Doo Wop and Jazz, along with the musical stylings of Frank Sinatra, Tony Bennett, Bing Crosby, and Nat King Cole.

The interesting and eclectic music was born, in part, from the heightening clashes between communism and capitalism and the beginnings of the space race, which had its origins with the United States and the Soviet Union; both nations building ballistic missiles which could be used to launch objects into space.[14] But even before the 1957 launch of Sputnik 1, the Russians made the first ever man-made satellite, people in the Sudbury region were continuing to see and report strange objects in the sky.

O.W. Saarinen writes in the book *Sudbury: Rail Town to Regional Capital*, that a five-year stockpiling contract to sell

SPOOKY SUDBURY

nickel and copper to the United States in 1953, along with the increased use of nickel by civilians, led to incredible growth and expansion of mining in the Sudbury Region.[15]

The industrial and population growth, which had been climbing in the 1940s already, reached incredible proportions, with a 1951 study and a Dominion Board of Statistics confirming that the gross density of population was approximately twenty persons per acre and with "42,410 jammed in 9,450 units," Sudbury had the reputation of being the most crowded city in Canada. Very little usable land remained in the city itself, which led to a move by many families into surrounding suburbs.[16]

With such overcrowding on the land, and a pioneering move in all outlying directions from the centre of the city, it was just another reason why residents of the region were starting to look up and thus notice things in the sky.

In February of 1950, C. Paquette, a Canadian Pacific Railroad (CPR) yardman in Cartier, witnessed an exploding star at 2:00 a.m. "All of a sudden," Paquette told the *Sudbury Daily Star*, "there was a flash as bright as lightning that showed on the ground and then bright fragments flew in all directions. It was just like a bursting skyrocket." Paquette's story was backed up by two other people, another yardman and a foreman.[17]

In March, twelve residents of Whitefish Falls reported peculiar silvery objects at three o'clock on a Saturday afternoon. The object was reported by a Mrs. R. Dow as round and "silvery white" in colour. "It was very high in the sky," she said, "It gave the appearance of moving up and down. Then to the right and left." Dow explained that it looked very different from a wayward balloon, which she had seen come to rest during the war. Eyewitnesses reported that it hovered for about an hour before moving so high that it was no longer visible.[18]

The 1950s: The Race To (and from) Space

Approximately a month later, in April, Arthur Penny of Sudbury reported a flying saucer moving at a rapid rate when he was on a stroll down Lansdowne Street. "It looked like two pie plates one on top of the other," he was quoted as saying in an April 17, 1950, article in the *Sudbury Star*. "It was smooth and about the size of a small washtub." Penny explained that a man on a bicycle pointed out the object in the sky. "I looked up and saw this thing spinning along. It went out of sight in the direction of Copper Cliff."

A similar report from an unidentified woman from Elm Street in Sudbury reported a "strange silvery-shaped disc affair" racing across the sky at approximately 6:30 a.m. She explained that the object seemed to appear out of the sky over Lake Ramsey, raced over Cedar and Larch Streets, then disappeared in a black cloud over the Pearl Street water tower.[19]

Later on that same month, a number of residents on the grounds at Lansdowne Public School witnessed what they described as a "huge hawk" flying at one hundred miles per hour at approximately six thousand feet. An Ontario Department of Lands and Forests employee named Milton Horn described the object as being as big as a tub and heading due north without a visible exhaust or lights. He and his wife, along with a small group of friends, claimed to have spotted the object that evening around 8:40 p.m.[20]

A few months passed before another incident was reported in the local papers. But during the civic holiday weekend Garson residents reported a pan-shaped object hovering in the sky in the late afternoon. One resident reported seeing a large object flying at about one thousand feet that afternoon, and later on two others saw a similar object at about 7:00 p.m. They vaguely described what they saw as saucer shaped, but provided no other details.[21]

SPOOKY SUDBURY

In November 1951, Walter Kottick, a local area plumber, reported that he and two passengers followed a mysterious flying object from Turbine, a settlement a little more than twenty miles west of the city. "We were just past the crossing at Turbine at 3:30 a.m. this morning when we saw it," Kottick explained to a reporter at the *Sudbury Daily Star*, "At first I thought it was an observation balloon. Then we saw it was a lot of different coloured lights. When we got as close as we could we put the spotlight from the car on it and it veered away and went up high."[22]

Kottick explained that he and his companions thought it might be a star, but then they witnessed it travelling on the right hand side of the road, then the left, then back to the right again, almost like a plane that was banking. He said they were driving approximately sixty miles an hour to try to catch up to it and that all three were stone cold sober. The Sudbury weather bureau was unable to identify the light, although did make note that there had been a report of an advertising balloon that got loose in Winnipeg and was last seen heading north. Interestingly, at about the time the balloon was reported to be lose, prevailing winds in the Sudbury region were east and southeast and thus could not carry the balloon in the direction of Sudbury, even if it were possible for the balloon to travel such as great distance in such a short time.[23] Within a couple of days of this report, an Espanola woman by the name of Shaughnessy was on her way home from bingo when she saw a flash of vivid blue lightning overtop of the KVP Plant, above the tall smoke stack. She explained that the flashes were in steady intervals and in the form of an over-sized beacon light shifting from side to side. Nobody, however, took her reports seriously, chalking it up to bingo night gossip that she enjoyed sharing.[24]

It wasn't until about a year later that a young boy looking for his cat at supper time claimed to have seen a strange light in the

THE 1950S: THE RACE TO (AND FROM) SPACE

sky, describing it as red and white, with fire coming out of one side. "There was no noise," he told the *Sudbury Daily Star*, "The fire zoomed across the sky and then dipped down low, up over the hills and out of sight." The boy, Robert Hastings, added that the object had been travelling at "a pretty good clip."[25]

One of the next sightings didn't occur until January 1953, when a Mrs. Russel Howard and three other individuals witnessed two silvery torpedo-shaped objects flying over Copper Cliff. They said that the two objects were moving very slowly across the sky toward the lake, making absolutely no sound as they disappeared from sight, and then reappeared all within a half hour time frame.[26] Just a few days after, Mrs. Howard and her friends witnessed the pair of silver sky torpedoes without wings, more reports started to flood in, confusing both local meteorologists and a Hanmer area Royal Canadian Air Force (RCAF) radio station spokesperson. A Mrs. Scaba also described seeing a pair of round, wingless shapes in the sky at about the same time, and a Mrs. Pullin witnessed one of the objects, describing it in a similar fashion and explaining how it moved toward the lake until she lost sight of it from around the side of her house.[27]

The RCAF later confirmed that a jet aircraft had been flying over Sudbury on the Thursday when these reports originated. Reports for a local police constable, Gene Kiviaho, and a civilian by the name of K. Morning correctly identified the RCAF reported jet that was in the sky at approximately the same time. The RCAF spokesperson said that the pilot of the jet had not reported any unusual activity from unidentified spacecraft. Interestingly, though, a separate report came in from William Kottick, the gentleman who had raced the flying saucer shapes along the side of the highway in November of 1951, describing something slightly different. Kottick reported seeing a white, cigar-shaped object navigating in a vertical direction in the air over Frood Mine.

Upon seeing it from his location at Baby's Garage on Frood Road, he called his wife, who looked out her back window and spotted the same object. She reported it as a cigar-shaped white cloud and that it was horizontal rather than vertical.[28]

Mrs. Foucault, the wife of a former air force instructor, also reported witnessing two shapes moving slowly southeast at a low altitude at about the same time. "They definitely weren't balloons or jets," Mrs. Foucault told the *Sudbury Daily Star*, "I have seen many weather balloons when my husband was stationed at various air force bases during the war. And there was nothing about them that resembled planes."[29]

Local residents Mrs. Luke, and Mr. and Mrs. Stewart added their reports not long after, making it the third time in less than two weeks that similarly strange sightings were made in the area. At about 9:15 p.m. on Friday, February 13, Mrs. Luke spotted from her home on the south shore of Lake Ramsey what she described as a pear-shaped red object that floated motionless for about twenty minutes. After the first ten minutes of looking at it, she contacted her neighbours, the Stewarts, who also witnessed the bizarre red light. Mr. Stewart described the light as being similar to the colour of a flare or railway fuse and that it was about the same size as the moon. After approximately twenty minutes from when it was first spotted, it disappeared.[30]

That same weekend, two other Sudbury residents reported a strange phenomenon in the sky to the west. Ed Zettler and Pete Bullock were leaving Bullock's house at about half past 7:00 p.m. when they spotted a crescent shape about the size of the moon, but obscured in a blue mist. They said that the object remained there for perhaps ten to fifteen seconds before it disappeared.[31] An independent report filed by Dave Parkatti substantiated the report of the two men. Parkatti, an Inco worker, said he had been standing on his mother's back porch when he noticed an

THE 1950s: THE RACE TO (AND FROM) SPACE

object in the sky to the west that reminded him of the search lights he saw in England during the war, except that there was no beam, just a "sort of dirty grey colour." Parkatti said that the phenomenon reminded him of the sun shining through thick cloud except for the grey colour.[32]

On Monday February 16, 1953, at approximately 11:00 p.m., just after her husband had left for his work shift, a Mrs. Burton reported seeing a glowing red object over Lake Ramsey. "I immediately saw this red glow over the lake," she reported, "and thought at first it was from the Coniston smelter." But then she realized as she watched it, suspended just over the horizon, that it was something different because it started to grow larger, stretch out, and change its position in the sky with a slight silvery appearance around the edges. Then it began to grow smaller again, the silver hue fading back to red.[33]

Just a little over a week later, both Mr. and Mrs. Burton saw something else in the sky, a different phenomenon, which leads a bit of credence to their tale. If the original account was fiction, one would think that they would have stuck with the same story. But the second incident is unique.

"My wife spotted them first," Mr. Burton said in an article printed in the *Sudbury Daily Star* on February 24, 1953, "And together we watched them through our front window. There appeared to be two silvery streaks, one above the other." He described them as being as far apart as each of them was wide and that a round silvery object trailed behind them.[34]

Burton said that the objects were moving slowly toward the north and then seemed to come together to form a round mass about one and a half times the diameter of the full moon, silver in colour and with vague blurry edges. "The big object then moved back to about the spot we had first seen it and gradually faded out."[35]

SPOOKY SUDBURY

Reports of objects in the sky were quiet for a few months, as it wasn't until April of that same year when the next documented case came in. On Sunday, April 12, half a dozen men from Coniston were heading toward Sudbury at about 10:00 p.m. when they witnessed a cigar-shaped object glowing above the mine. It hovered there for about twenty minutes, not moving but changing in shape and colour.[36]

When the men first spotted the object over the mine, it was pinkish-red and shaped like a cigar or pencil. After a few minutes it began to glow white and shrunk down to the size of a dime. Then, after another ten minutes it turned red again and stretched out to the original cigar shape.[37]

A few months later, Burton Avenue residents witnessed a bright flying object about the size of an orange coming in from the north sky, travelling at a high altitude and a slow speed. It reportedly trailed a foot-long flame which shimmered in colour between light blue to dull red. The noiseless object hovered overhead before turning at a sharp angle and heading west, then disappeared into the northeast sky.[38]

The rest of that year was quiet with respect to UFO and strange light sightings. In fact, Sudbury went through the remainder of that fall as well as the full winter and spring season without any of the reports that had become typical and almost expected. But that "dry period" was made up for in spades in July with the report of alien visitors.

On the same day that Mars was closer to the earth than it had ever been before, Friday, July 2, 1954, Ennio La Sorza, an employee of Garson Mine, claimed to have been visited by three thirteen-foot alien visitors with hypnotic powers.[39]

La Sorza arrived at the first aid station white as a ghost and fainted immediately. When he awoke he told the story of seeing three giant aliens, likely from Mars, he said, descending from

The 1950s: The Race To (and from) Space

a twenty-five-foot diameter space ship that had two electronic ear-like spurs on its "head" and three sets of arms with claws and six legs. He described the centre of the ship as square with a telescopic projection, and stated that the alien men were built in a similar manner to the telescopic protrusion.[40]

La Sorza claimed he saw the three creatures descend from portholes in the side of the spacecraft that, only moments earlier, had been hovering like a helicopter twenty-five feet above the ground. He began to run, but one of the three creatures froze him to the spot and emitted a telepathic message to him through its single eye. "I'd rather be dead than carry out the message I was given," La Sorza was reported to have said. "It was horrible."[41]

He was uncertain as to whether or not the aliens had actually spoken aloud to him. But one thing that was certain was the ripple of fear and rumours that kept people afraid to go out after dark for fear of encountering "the monster."[42]

Reverend Charles Beck, a Buffalo-area radio preacher, visited Sudbury shortly after to investigate La Sorza's claim, and explained that Sudbury was likely to be in for plenty more visits from alien visits. "Your town is to be the centre of flying saucer activity because of the nickel mines here," Beck told Sudbury reporters. "Saucers are interested in anything progressive. They are interested in atomic energy and any kind of mines."[43]

Beck went on to make further claims about the saucer people. "They are observing you. In fact, the saucers are here now. There are many saucer people here now. They are walking your streets, mingling with your people here, even in your plants. They know every word between your officials." He added that they have the ability to change shape, become invisible, and walk through solid objects.

Beck outlined similarities between the reports made by La Sorza at the Garson Mine and something that happened two

SPOOKY SUDBURY

years earlier in Flatwoods, West Virginia. A solider followed two youngsters who had reported seeing a flying saucer land in the woods, to discover a fifteen-foot-tall creature with a greenish-blue body, a reddish face, six pincer-tipped arms, and six legs.[44]

After this rather startling and pretty "progressive" report, the rest of the summer remained relatively quiet on the flying saucer and Martian invader front.

It wasn't until September that various reports of UFO sightings of a "glowing ball," "circular shaped" objects, and "white discs" appeared in nearby Timmins and North Bay.[45, 46,.47]

By the end of September, a new and decidedly different UFO was reported in Sudbury. This time, instead of a circular, oval, or cigar shape, the shape reported was a triangle.

At about 9:40 p.m. on Sunday, September 19, Mr. and Mrs. Peter Showdra were visiting relatives on Burwash road in Sudbury and saw an object with a triangular front of a bright yellowish colour travelling at a "terrific velocity and altitude." They claimed the object was visible for a little over five minutes before it came to a sudden stop and disappeared. About half an hour later, the same object became visible once more and then flashed in and out of the visible spectrum for several minutes.[48]

The following couple of years saw a string of flying saucers in Cobalt (near Lake Temiskaming), Kirkland Lake, and Cache Bay.[49, 50] But the next significant report of UFO sightings closer to Sudbury didn't come until the spring of 1956.

This time, with a heightened sense of the Cold War mounting, the newspaper articles of the day referenced the reported objects as potential evidence of a "Russian" threat, indicating a conflation of people's fears of being invaded not only by aliens from another planet, but humans from the other side of the world.

An article dated March 31, 1956, in the *Sudbury Daily Star* begins with the following question: "Could it be Russians are

The 1950s: The Race To (and from) Space

infiltrating Canada's radar defences and coming close enough to study the activities of the Nickel Capital of the World?" The article goes on to outline two different reports of flying saucers in the area, described as "a ball of fire in the sky" by one pair of observers and as "a bright silvery" pencil-shaped streak that was vertical at first and then turned horizontal. These individual accounts were reported northwest of Garson.[51]

The year 1957 saw a string of reports in the late summer/ early fall season, with two fifteen-year-old astronomers reporting watching a "bright light with a tail" for more than half an hour on a Sunday night, and then again the following night. But the astronomers in question (Clifford Walton and George Hartman) were clear to denote their belief that what they had been looking at had been comets. [52, 53] Other similar reports from the remainder of the year seemed to be similarly informed, as a "mysterious" bright light in the southwest sky was explained as possibly being Venus, and a "fireball" or "very bright star" might very well have been a meteor.[54, 55]

In April 1958, Con Kelly reported sighting a bright light moving across the sky, from the direction of Sudbury General Hospital toward Coniston, at around 8:00 p.m. on a Saturday night. It was discussed as possibly being a sighting of Sputnik, the first manmade object sent into orbit by Russia. However, as pointed out by officials at the Toronto area Dunlap Observatory, the sighting was too early for Sputnik's scheduled trip over top of Northern Ontario.

It is interesting to note that, at about the time that Sputnik was launched, the thought of man being capable of "space flight" and sending man-made objects seemed to have the effect of reducing the number of "flying saucer" sightings. With aircraft and jet advances becoming more "commonplace" as the 1950s were ending, people could also be more likely to consider that the lights and objects they saw in the sky were, in fact, the

SPOOKY SUDBURY

result of man-made objects. The Sudbury Airport, for example, opened in 1952, which naturally led to an increase in witnesses reporting seeing objects in the sky that were "known" rather than "unidentified" flying objects.[56]

One of the last reports of a strange object in the sky from the Sudbury Region comes from an experienced sky watcher. After hearing about a report of a ball of fire over the skies in Wahnapitae on Friday July 18, 1958, by Joe Gariepy, Paul Drisdell of Levack, a member of the Royal Astronomical Society of Canada, reported seeing something similar the previous week.[57]

On July 8, Drisdell was on his Hemlock Street home in Levack and watching the sky through a telescope when, at approximately 10:30 p.m., he witnessed an "unfamiliar object" angle across the sky moving from the western to the southern sky.

"It was very bright and ten times the magnitude of Jupiter," Drisdell explained to the *Sudbury Daily Star*. I've been watching the sky for five years now, and I never before saw anything like this." He explained that he couldn't get a closer look at it because it had been moving too fast to track using his telescope.

Familiar with astrological movements, Drisdell confirmed checking that it could not have been a meteor because the next meteor shower was not expected for another eight days. "I'm certain it wasn't a meteor," Drisdell said. "I've seen plenty of them, and they don't look anything like this thing did. It went slower than a meteor and kept a steady course without winking."

Drisdell stated he understood that air force pilots could identify an aircraft in one-tenth of a second, and that, because he had been tracking the object for at least five full seconds, he had plenty of time to study it and was pretty sure that it was not a natural manifestation.

When the 1950s began, Sudbury was one of the fastest growing cities in Canada. The fifties were, in the words of O.W.

THE 1950s: THE RACE TO (AND FROM) SPACE

Saarinen, years of "growth, prosperity and unbridled optimism for the city."[58] But they were also part of a time that was still recovering from a major World War, was continuing to face conflicts, the growing un-nerving threat of the Cold War, advances in technology such as passenger jet service, man-made satellites, and hydrogen bomb testing. Combine this tension with the unprecedented growth and population explosion faced by this small but bustling northern community, and it is not surprising that folks were continuing to look toward the skies to spot and take note of bizarre and interesting objects.

The 1960s: Did You Detect That Movement in the Sky?

The Sixties were a period of counter-culture, social revolution, and even further political and technological advances. From the Vietnam War to the anti-war movement; from the assassination of John F. Kennedy to the legendary "I have a dream" speech by Martin Luther King Jr.; from the first human footsteps on the moon to Timothy Leary's "Turn on, tune in, drop out" slogan; from Trudeaumania to Quebec separatism; this decade can be summed up in Dickens' classic opening line "It was the best of times, it was the worst of times."

While the Rolling Stones hit number one because of their inability to get any satisfaction, Simon and Garfunkel were revelling in the sound of silence. And while Elvis returned to civilian and stage life from a stint in the army, Motown Record Corporation was founded. And as The Doors, The Beatles, The Beach Boys, Bob Dylan, and The Supremes were rocking the charts, the song "Sudbury Saturday Night" was written by Stompin' Tom Connors and performed at the Towne House — a song that would continue to be an ongoing weekly anthem depicting the hard-working, hard-rocking, and hard-drinking city and its people.

THE 1960s: DID YOU DETECT THAT MOVEMENT IN THE SKY?

In Sudbury, the sixties were a period of turmoil and unrest. As the two major mining companies (Inco and Falconbridge) were expanding their operations, political struggles between union groups such as the International Union of Mine, Mill and Smelter Workers, the United Steelworkers Union, and mine management resulted in wildcat strikes and the Ontario Provincial Police bringing in helicopters, police dogs, and mace to quell picket line violence. This political unrest of the sixties created an atmosphere of uncertainty, tension and anxiety.[59, 60]

And it wasn't enough that the uncertainly lay in the politics and the social movements of the time; there was continued uncertainty about the possibility of invaders either from another country or another planet — one could, of course, never be sure.

In July of 1960, a pair of high school students, Susan McGruther and Huguette Beaucheme, reported seeing a large unidentified object at approximately 8:00 p.m. on Tuesday July 12, while they were vacationing at a camp on Long Lake. "There were no clouds in the sky and the round silver object was too large for a star," McGruther reported. "It didn't look anything like an airplane. I never saw anything like it before."[61] A similar object, described like a large white shining beach ball, was seen by two other girls in November of that same year.[62]

On Thursday February 9, 1961, multiple reports came in of a craft hovering in the sky just west of Murray Mine, from both workers at that mine and a trio in a car. The driver of the vehicle, a young man by the name of Charles Meyes, reported actually being chased by the object around midnight. According to the report, the bright round object, which alternated between a bright white and red light and was about the size of a car roof, was hovering about fifty to sixty feet above the ground, following the vehicle with the three men inside, stopping when they stopped and continuing on when they resumed their journey.

This continued for several minutes as they moved along Highway 17, until they reached the city limits and they reported the object veered off into the distance.[63] The same object returned again on the Friday, and the same miners who had reported it the night before, saw it again, describing it as less bright than on the previous sighting. A couple living on nearby Vermillion River reported seeing a bright, wobbly light, orange in colour, moving slowly through the sky and lighting up their darkened living room.[64]

A similar object was reported again the following night by a motorist and his wife, on Highway 17 between Verner and Hagar, who had no idea of the previous reports. The unnamed couple described an unidentified object that seemed to match the reports made on the preceding nights. "We thought it must be a helicopter," the male motorist said, describing the far off dim object that appeared about a mile off and, becoming brighter

UFOs were regularly seen over lonely stretches of highways.

THE 1960S: DID YOU DETECT THAT MOVEMENT IN THE SKY?

with a red sheen as it moved closer. "But no helicopter could do what it was doing. There must be some explanation." The motorist did not speculate as to why the object, which travelled a parallel route to their vehicle, continually dipping and passing their vehicle, did not appear to make any sound whatsoever.[65]

Many reports from that same time of objects in the sky were provided by people who seemed to know the difference, when reporting strange lights, between "Sputniks" (a term which seemed to have been regularly used to describe objects understood to be man-made satellites in the sky) and other unidentifiable flying objects.

In September 1961, three police officers and a civilian reported seeing a pair of strange objects over the Number 3 shaft of Creighton Mine at about eight o'clock in the morning on Friday the 15th. Although there were no reports of detectable objects from the radar station at Falconbridge, perhaps because the objects were too close to the equipment, the objects were reported as each being as big as a house and flying in parallel formation approximately one hundred yards apart. "As we were watching them," Constable Ray Phillon said, "they seemed to take off in a jerky motion." Phillon described them as at perhaps two thousand feet in altitude and appearing larger at the base than at the top, with no visible windows or ports.[66]

Reports in the following five years were scant, with another sighting of a bright orange light arching in the sky from west to east, moving at a constant speed without any sort of burning tail coming in January of 1966. This sighting was one that could not be explained by the RCAF radar base at Falconbridge.[67]

In Elliot Lake in March, a pair of astronomy students reported seeing an orange, glowing object suddenly appear within a constellation known as "the belt of the hunter" before it stopped, changed to a vivid blue colour, and moved again, before

SPOOKY SUDBURY

fading to a yellowish-brown colour and then disappearing into the northern sky.[68]

The summer and fall of 1967 were filled with further unidentified flying object reports, from a fast-moving series of flashing red, green and blue lights that seemed to disappear behind the moon,[69] to a reported near-landing of a UFO bearing green coloured lights in a Whitefish field, accompanied by a whining sound that blacked out a young man's portable transistor radio.[70]

In November of that same year, a group of five people reported seeing an unidentified flying object hover in the early morning sky south of the Kingsway and near Falconbridge Road for about ten minutes. The object was described as ten to fifteen times larger than a star and with bright changing colours (a luminous white to a bright green).[71] And less than a month later, a self-proclaimed UFO watcher reported seeing three elongated objects, not unlike florescent lights in shape, floating over the western horizon.[72]

And, in a report that seems quite similar to an incident from 1961, two young men were tracked by a silver-coloured object with flashing red lights that stopped when they stopped, and resumed moving when they continued to drive along, until it finally seemed to grow tired of the chase and disappeared. At around the same time, two other young men, this time high school students from Nickel District Collegiate, reported being scared out of their wits when a silver craft with flashing lights appeared twenty feet above their car, causing their engine to die completely.[73]

The major local claim of capturing a flying object on film came from five Laurentian University students at the beginning of 1968. Jim Lockett, Larry Coutts, Jim Calarco, Stan Wallace and Dyck Cybulski were setting up a camera for night pictures of the University of Sudbury residence for the Laurentian University yearbook when a strange light appeared in the sky.[74]

The 1960s: Did You Detect that Movement in the Sky?

"I didn't know what it was," Calarco said, when he saw the light coming slowly from the west. "I yelled to everyone."[75]

The white disc shaped light hovered in the sky over Nepahwin Lake for about four minutes, eerily making no detectable sound at all. Jim Lockett, a second-year arts student and photo editor for the yearbook, had time to snap about a dozen pictures using the thirty-five mm camera before the object suddenly got smaller and smaller, seeming to move away from the golf course where the young men were standing, until it completely disappeared.[76]

A picture of the object, what one might think of as a typical flying saucer, that was taken that night, appeared in the *Sudbury Daily Star* on January 24, 1968, along with a photo of Coutts, Calarco, and Lockett holding the photo.[77]

More strange silver objects were reported in the skies in August 1968, over Sudbury[78] and Elliot Lake,[79] but the culmination of the sixties came with a sighting in conjunction with an event that was widely witnessed and celebrated.

In July of 1969, during the same week when most of the world was glued to their television sets watching Neil Armstrong and his companions taking their first steps on the moon, three Sudbury-area men had their eyes fixed to the local skies. The men, Jack Sonnenberg, Edmond Sonnenberg, and Bob Melcher, were travelling home from work near the Allen Fergusson farm, when they encountered a blinding red light. The light was so bright that the driver had to slam on the brakes. They sat stunned in the car and watched the bright moon-shaped object head west, blink a few times, and then disappear off into the sky.[80]

As the light disappeared into the sky, the three men tried to make heads or tails of what they had just witnessed. At the same time, the world was still adjusting to President Kennedy's declaration that the U.S. would put a man on the moon by the close of the decade.

SPOOKY SUDBURY

Of course, understanding humanity's ability to venture into space led true believers to speculate that alien civilizations could also have technologies even more advanced than ours, and be visiting Earth with either the same exploratory goals as ours, or perhaps with more ulterior motives.

THE 1970S: THE SCRAMBLE OVER FALCONBRIDGE

The 1970s were another tumultuous decade; it saw a continuation of the Cold War, the end of the Vietnam War, a major oil and energy crisis, U.S. president Richard Nixon being charged with impeachment for the Watergate scandal, and a religious-based cult led by Jim Jones that ended with the people of Jonestown being led to or forced to drink a cyanide-laced fruit punch that left nine hundred of them dead.

On the progressive side of things, the civil rights and feminism movements brought positive change to societies, while technology introduced the first hand-held scientific calculator, the VCR, the Sony Walkman, and microwave ovens.

Musical highlights included progressive rock bands Led Zepplin, The Who, Pink Floyd, Supertramp, Rush, Genesis, and Yes. The decade also saw the loss of such notable musical talent as Jimi Hendrix, Janis Joplin, Jim Morrison, Bing Crosby, and the King, Elvis Presley.

Despite the mini-recession facing Canada, Sudbury's economy was still booming — thanks to the two mines (Inco and Falconbridge), which accounted for fifty percent of the

SPOOKY SUDBURY

city's employment.[81] In an attempt to make up for the strikes of 1969, the mines raised production speed. INCO's output in 1970 was one and a half times what it had been two years earlier, but that same year brought an average of one death per month. Inquests into the rising death toll pointed at poor training and the circumvention of training regulations by workers who were more interested in the carrot of the bonus pay than enforcing safety regulations.[82] By the mid 1970s, the economic boom turned into a bust, resulting in more miner strikes, reminiscent of those which occurred during the turbulent decade of the 60s.[83]

The year 1971 saw Apollo 14 bringing astronauts to the moon, the launch of the Voyager's exploratory spacecraft, and America's first space station, Skylab. But after the first couple of moon landings, the general public had lost most of their interest in following the developments of NASA.

However, even while the general public's interest in space exploration was waning, their interest in looking toward the heavens for unidentified flying objects, and the accompanying alien visitors was still as solid as it had ever been.

The early 1970s saw multiple reports of a round silver coloured object in the night sky over Hanmer, as well as a giant red ball the size of the moon that made a sound like whirring helicopter blades. That period also included witnesses spying a big red circling object in the skies over Whitefish and at least five different people at the Sudbury General Hospital reporting seeing a bright silver oval-shaped object moving in the sky across Lake Ramsey.[84, 85, 86, 87]

One of the most interesting ongoing series of reports come from nearby Manitoulin Island, and a run of a series of consecutive nights where a Manitoulin teen by the name of John Dunlop, a thirteen-year-old who did not previously believe in

The 1970s: The Scramble Over Falconbridge

Thirteen-year-old John Dunlop reported strange oval-shaped objects in the sky over Sheguiandah Bay in Manitoulin.

UFOs, spotted a strange oval-shaped aircraft with flashing lights that hovered, landed in the bay, and could travel a mile within two seconds.[88]

Dunlop's reports included the first night in which he saw the bright oval-shaped object in the eastern sky and tracked its movements, picking out the red, green, yellow, and orange flashing lights before watching it settle down near Ten-Mile Point on Sheguindah Bay.[89]

Newspaper reporters spent an evening with the boy, attempting to personally witness one of the repeated sightings, but, despite the object having appeared brightly in the clear sky on the day before, that night, nothing was seen.[90]

Even though the Sudbury reporters were unable to spot anything out of the ordinary when accompanying the thirteen-year-old, at least three other witnesses to those strange lights in

SPOOKY SUDBURY

the sky stepped forward to report their own individual sight-ings.[91] Additional sightings were reported by both Dunlop and another young boy the following week,[92] and just a few days later, making it the tenth sighting in so many days, Dunlop reported seeing that same strange flying object hovering in the distance about one thousand feet in the air, flashing red and yellow lights, before speeding off and disappearing.[93]

It is one thing, of course, to rely on civilian reports of unex-plained lights and objects in the sky, but yet another when the reports are corroborated by radar technology, local police constables, and air force personnel. But that is exactly what hap-pened just a few months after the series of reports that came from Manitoulin.

On the morning of Tuesday November 11, 1975, at approxi-mately 4:50 a.m., regional police constables Alex Keable and Bob Whiteside spotted three objects in the sky. In order to get a bet-ter look, they drove their vehicle over to Logan avenue, where they determined that there were actually four objects of varying brightness and demonstrating different movements. While one of the objects remained stationary, others, like the one they spot-ted in the southwest sky, appeared to jerk and slide. The objects remained visible until they went off duty a little more than two hours later.[94]

Officer John Marsh, a patrolman on Highway 17 East near Coniston, reported seeing a similar pulsating jerking light in the southwest sky. At around the same time, two other offices reported an object lighting up the clouds in the western part of the city. Able to get their hands on binoculars, Constables Gary Chrapynski and J.B. Deighton reported a cylindrical bright object that remained until after the sun had risen in the eastern sky.[95]

That same day, an officer in Dowling reported that he fol-lowed a bright object down Highway 144 and Errington Street

THE 1970S: THE SCRAMBLE OVER FALCONBRIDGE

in Chelmsford and in Haileybury, a town more than one hundred miles east, a similar bright object was reported over Lake Timiskaming.[96]

At least four different people at the radar station in Falconbridge tracked the UFOs on their radars, they spotted three bright circles with dark dots and photographed the objects. National Defence Headquarters in Ottawa confirmed that the UFOs picked up on the radar were moving between 42,000 and 72,000 feet.[97]

A public information officer from NORAD named Del Kindschi confirmed from Colorado Springs that something had indeed been tracked on the radar in Sudbury and a squadron of U.S. Air National Guard F-106 interceptors took off from the U.S. Air Force base at Selfridge, Michigan, a little after 12:00 p.m. to scan and inspect the skies over Sudbury. The jet fighter pilots did not find anything when they arrived, but by then it had already been several hours since the objects had last been sighted.[98]

The reports in Sudbury were part of a broader series of incidents that had been documented over Sudbury and North Bay, as well as Montana, Michigan, Maine, New Brunswick, and Newfoundland, placing several Strategic Air Command bases in the northern tier states on high alert. The repeated and consistent intrusions of radar-confirmed unidentified flying aircraft flying at low altitude over atomic weapons storage areas made authorities a bit too uncomfortable.[99]

The UFO Casebook website revealed the following NORAD regional director logs with time expressed in Greenwich Mean Time (GMT) or "Zebra" (Z) Time. They were obtained by Larry Fawcett and Barry Greenwood:

1205 GMT. "Unusual sighting report" made.

SPOOKY SUDBURY

1840 GMT. Jet interceptors were scrambled, airborne at 1750Z "due to unusual object sighting ... UFO report from Falconbridge."

At 0202GMT on November 15, 1975, "Report sent to NCOC Surveillance, referred to Assistant Command Director Space Defense Center, and intelligence. These 3 individuals considered the report a UFO report and not an unknown track report."[100]

Similarly, the NORAD report was also quoted on the UFO Casebook website:

Falconbridge reported [at 4:05 a.m.] search and height finder paints [radar targets] on an object 25 to 30 nautical miles south of the site ranging in altitude from 26,000 feet to 72,000 feet [appearing visually as like a bright star]. With binoculars, the object appeared as a 100-ft. diameter sphere and appeared to have craters [sic] around the outside ... To date, efforts by Air Guard helicopters, SAC helicopters and NORAD F-106s have failed to provide positive identification.[101]

On November 13, 1975, NORAD issued a press release. The following is quoted from the 2006 Dundurn book by Chris A. Rutkowski and Geoff Dittman, *The Canadian UFO Report: The Best Cases Revealed*:

At 4:05 p.m., Nov. 11, the Canadian Forces radar site at Falconbridge, Ontario, reported a radar track of an unidentified flying object about 25–30 nautical miles south of the site, ranging in altitude from 25,000 to

THE 1970S: THE SCRAMBLE OVER FALCONBRIDGE

72,000 feet. Persons at the site also saw the object and said it appeared as a bright star but much closer. Two F-106 aircraft of the US Air Force Air National Guard's 171st Fighter Interceptor Squadron at Selfridge ANGB, Michigan, were scrambled, but the pilots reported no contact with the object.[102]

After the jets surveyed the area, reported their lack of findings and left, reports from later that same day also surfaced, from both civilians who reported several objects in the sky between 10:00 p.m. and midnight, and two officers, who detected a lighted blinking object at around 2:00 a.m. on Highway 69.[103]

Interestingly, authors Rutkowski and Dittman point out in their coverage of the incident in *The Canadian UFO Report* that this incident involving Falconbridge and NORAD took place within the context of a significant wave of UFO reports across North America. A gigantic wave of reports that occurred shortly after NBC aired *The UFO Incident*, a dramatic recreation of a well-publicized Barney and Betty Hill UFO abduction incident. According to Phil Klass, a UFO-skeptic, the airing of that show was followed by three weeks of "an abnormal number of reports of sightings of unidentified objects in the sky."[104]

Hype and speculation in the human mind are, of course, one thing — but no manner of media or network television hysteria can make objects appear on radar, or result in a stringent and powerful entity such as the U.S. Air Force to take the immediate investigative actions that they did.

One thus wonders what really and truly happened in the skies over Falconbridge that Remembrance Day in 1975, details that remain classified and left un-reported to the public.

THE 1980s AND BEYOND: WHEREFORE ART THOU?

Technological innovations continued to grow in popularity as well as appear in more homes as the 1980s arrived, with portable music players, personal computers, and specialized television channels (such as MTV or the Canadian Much Music), dominating much of popular culture. Video arcades introduced such enduring characters as Pac Man, Frogger, and Mario Brothers. Michael Jackson's moonwalk captured the hearts and minds of people around the world and the highest-grossing movies included such "space-centric" blockbusters as *ET: The Extra Terrestrial, Star Wars* (*The Empire Strikes Back* and *Return of the Jedi*), the 1986 *Aliens* (a follow-up to Ridley Scott's 1979 film *Alien*) and the Arnold Schwarzenegger films *Predator* and *The Terminator*.

Looking up and towards space, the 1980s saw the arrival of Halley's Comet and the advent of the Space Shuttle program, which, sadly, included the January 1986 loss of six astronauts and the first civilian in space when the space shuttle *Challenger* exploded seconds after lift off.

As C.M. Wallace wrote in chapter eleven of the book *Sudbury: Rail Town to Regional Capital*, (the chapter that focused on the

The 1980s and Beyond: Wherefore Art Thou?

1980s), "The 1980s began with an obituary." Wallace describes the city when the decade began as a falling and failing city which had succumbed to an inevitable fate; the fate associated with towns built upon particular resources.[105]

However, as Wallace continues to explore in that same chapter, by the time the decade ended, Sudbury was again prosperous, while the rest of Canada and North America was facing a recession. Like in 1971, when the Apollo astronauts visited the region to explore the 1.8 billion-year-old meteorite crater that formed the Nickel District, outside experts returned to study and understand how this northern town could defy elemental logic.[106]

Wallace outlines various developments in Sudbury that added additional layers to the mining town, including the establishment and growth of the Sudbury Theatre Centre's new building, with a capacity for more than four thousand subscribers.[107]

Sudbury saw another significant cultural destination, Science North, open on June 19, 1984 (it was later "officially opened" by Queen Elizabeth II and Prince Philip in October of that same year).[108] This northern destination, with a unique hands-on approach to science, helped inject life into the cultural scene by presenting science as fun, interesting, and engaging. The stated mission of Science North involves "high-quality science education and entertainment experiences which involve people in the relationship between science and everyday life."[109]

In a spirit similar to that which drives Science North, local ufologist Michel Deschamps has dedicated himself to researching and sharing unique findings related to UFO sightings in Northern Ontario. Deschamps, who saw his first UFO, a circular ball-like object hovering in the sky over Hanmer when he was nine years old, has always been interested in UFO sightings.[110]

Michel Deschamps's Northern Ontario UFO Research and Study (NOUFORS) website contains almost four hundred news-

The snowflake design of Science North makes it appear, to some, like a flying saucer that has landed on a Ramsey Lake rock cut.

paper clippings regarding UFO sightings in Northern Ontario, dozens of recorded interviews with witnesses and hundreds of first person accounts from 1995 to 2013. Deschamps's site also contains thousands of links and scanned documents released as part of the *Freedom of Information Act (FOIA)* the Federal Bureau of Investigation (FBI), the Central Intelligence Agency (CIA), the National Security Agency (NSA) and the Defense Intelligence Agency (DIA). Deschamps also includes *Communications Instructions Reporting Vital Intelligence Sightings (CIRVIS)* documents as made available through to Canada's version of FOIA, *Canada's Access to Information Law.*

As evidenced through the NOUFORS website, the incidents of UFO sightings, while nowhere near as heavily reported in local print media as it was in the fifties, sixties, and seventies, continue to this day.

With an extensive archive of personal reports as gathered between 1995 and today, Deschamps has taken the care to collect, clip, scan, and provide full access to interested readers of all

THE 1980S AND BEYOND: WHEREFORE ART THOU?

unidentified object sightings (from meteors to undeterminable aircraft to reports of alien encounters). Among the most startling (and recent) are reports of hovering, darting, and blinking lights in the skies over Wahnapitae, reported on March 4, 2013, as well as three strange round objects shooting off sparks reported from four witnesses near Sudbury Downs in Azilda.[111]

As reported by CBC's Steve Puddicombe on March 7, 2013, with the continuing government cutbacks, it is very unlikely that any further funding will be made for the investigation of UFOs, leaving the task to "ordinary citizens and those with a keen scientific interest in the unexplained."[112]

The diligent nature of dedicated people such as Michel Deschamps, as well as author-researchers like Chris Rutkowski, author of *The Canadian UFO Report, The Big Book of UFOs*, and the ufology website will help to continue to document the continuing occurrences of people looking into our skies and seeing things that simply cannot be explained.

Do You Hear What I See?

The following story was submitted to us shortly after an article appeared in the *Sudbury Star* mentioning *Spooky Sudbury* and that there was still room to include more stories if there happened to be anything out there that someone wanted to share.

Carol, whose last name is being withheld to protect her privacy and the privacy of her family, related a tale of something that happened to her mother and father when she was quite young. A story that continues to intrigue her.

We lived in a community of eleven houses and had a lot of bush behind our yard. This was at our house out on Highway 17. It was fairly isolated and far enough away from the standard city noises.

My mother was putting some clothes out on the line when she looked in the distance and saw a strange saucer-shaped machine in the sky, a "machine." That is how she described the saucer-shaped craft, like it was some odd object; not an airplane or glider or anything like that — but a machine.

Do You Hear What I See?

She called out to my dad, who was in the nearby garage. He came out, curious to see what was going on and what the yelling and all the noise was all about.

She kept pointing to the saucer in the sky that was as clear as day, she had told me.

"There it is," she had said to him. "There it is! There! Don't you see it?"

My dad shook his head. "No," he said, seeing only a clear blue and cloudless sky. "I don't see anything. Which is strange, because I can certainly hear something." He was confused as to where the noise was coming from and described the loud machine-like noise ringing in his ears.

They stood looking at each other, completely baffled at how she could be seeing something that he wasn't able to see, despite how clear the vision was to her; and he was curious as to how she couldn't hear that incessant humming and whirring machine sound.

When the incident was over, and the sight and sound were gone, they were still puzzled and unsure at what they had just experienced. My mom called the newspaper and told a few people about the odd experience, but everybody she had told just laughed at her.

She figured people thought she might be crazy, so she never spoke about it publicly again.

I must have been in my early teens, maybe younger at that time; though I wasn't in the yard when that incident took place — it was just something that my mom relayed to me afterward. I'm now fifty-four years old and it seems to me this incident might have taken place in the 1960s. (And, no, my parents never took drugs, so this couldn't have been any sort of side-effect from an LSD trip.)

I have always been fascinated by my mother's story but she

165

SPOOKY SUDBURY

still doesn't want to want to talk about it. I do know it frightened her quite a bit.

My mom and dad are still living and are now in their 80s. The last time I spoke to her about it my mother sort of fluffed it off. This is completely unlike any other story my mother has ever told — she has never tried to tell anything that would seem to be so strange or unbelievable.

All I know is that ever since she told me that story I have always had a great curiosity about outer space.

I'm not sure what took place that day, nor why my dad couldn't see the object in the sky and why my mom couldn't hear the sound it was making.

But a story like this makes me believe we are not alone.

THE HUNTER AND THE HUNTED

Growing up in a small northern Ontario mining community like Levack, where one is surrounded by bountiful wilderness — a virtual utopia of lakes, rivers, rolling hills and trees — hunting and fishing is often a way of life.

For Levack residents, Thanksgiving is a special time of year, not merely for the gathering of families, the lavish turkey meals, the official celebration of the harvest, and all other things to be thankful for, but because it also heralds in moose hunting season for Northeastern Ontario.

There are many significant milestones in a man's life — however, in Levack, like in many Sudbury area communities, the significant ones of the 1970s included getting your first snowmobile licence, putting on your first local hockey team jersey (typically a white and blue Mine Mill or orange and white United Steelworkers sponsored one), and getting your gun licence, your fishing licence and your deer and moose hunting licences.

Brian Purvis celebrated the acquisition of his first moose hunting licence back in 1975, along with his friends Brian Deziel and Chummy White. The three, who had long planned and looked

SPOOKY SUDBURY

forward to their trip, had packed up and set off on a hunting trip in the vast lush forests behind the Inco and Falconbridge mine locations, popular spots for local hunters.

When the trio reached an appropriate-looking spot, they set up Purvis's tent trailer near a small lake, unpacked their supplies and prepared themselves for an early rise the next day; the day in which hunting season officially began and the three had very much been looking forward to.

As the three set up their camp area, Purvis paused to enjoy the cool nip in the air and to relish the feeling he had become used to; the bitter-sweet sensation that came with the reminder summer was long past, announced in the glorious splendour of the cavalcade of rich colours; the yellows, reds, and oranges that graced the trees.

There was, of course, a little something more in the air for Brian Purvis that year; an element undetectable to most, but which ran quite powerfully through him. This, being his very first moose hunting trip, signified a different type of passage, a rite experienced by so many men in his life and a heritage that he was now a part of. Purvis imagined this milestone event would be something he would always cherish and remember.

Little did he know, of course, that this particular trip, which ended up being his first and last moose hunting expedition, would be remembered for an entirely unexpected reason.

As darkness quickly descended upon the campsite, the way it seems to sneak up on a person when they drop their guard for just a moment, the three sat around playing cards, chatting and joking, their laughs and exuberance echoing across the serene and silent lake. They were having one of those special moments that men often look back to fondly, years later, recalling the carefree and joyous time spent with good pals — moments enjoyed while they were occurring, but recalled

THE HUNTER AND THE HUNTED

as something a bit more golden in nature when reminiscing about it decades after.

Eventually, the laughter quieted, the card game came to a conclusion, and the men extinguished the two propane lanterns and each crawled into their sleeping bags to settle down and rest for the early morning ahead. Despite the laughter and fun they were having, it didn't take long before even the brief chatter after lights out quelled and their breathing each slowed and they, one by one, gave themselves over to the shroud of sleep.

After an indeterminable time, Purvis woke to the unsettling sound; the voice of one of his buddies — who, he still isn't quite sure — cutting through the darkness and rousing him from sleep.

"What the hell is that?"

Purvis's eyes shot open and, though he knew it must have still been the middle of the night — there was no way that the men had been sleeping more than a few hours — he was immediately surprised at how bright it was inside the tent trailer. It was as if it were being lit from outside by a bright midday sun. It was at that point Brian also noted the loud and ominous thrumming sound in the air — something he thought might be a helicopter or perhaps even a low-flying jet.

He threw the flap of his sleeping bag aside and quickly slipped into his boots, while Chummy and Brian were doing the same. The three spilled out of the trailer and into an intense bright white light. Though it had seemed like daylight from inside the tent trailer, they now saw that it was a clear and artificially bright white light that seemed to be coming from somewhere above — not a single spot, but an overall glow. They couldn't actually see anything, due to the harsh light shining down, but Purvis distinctly remembers looking at his friends and at the trees and bushes adjacent to the campsite. The entire ground, the whole area around them was lit up from the bright light shining down from above.

169

Spooky Sudbury

Elapsed time exposure; conceptual "ghost" campfire photo.

Even shielding their eyes, they couldn't see anything other than the light. They stood there, alternating between trying to spot what was in the sky above them and glancing at one another, the loud thrumming vibrating through them as they stood there completely confused as to what was happening.

Then, almost immediately, the intense thrumming sound ceased and the light blinked out.

While the three men stood there, completely aghast, their eyes desperately trying to readapt to the dark night, they heard the sound of what seemed like the largest flock of geese any of them had ever heard landing on the small lake. The three knew the "fast clucking" sound that geese tend to make upon landing on the water, only the volume and intensity was louder than anything they had ever heard.

The Hunter and the Hunted

The three stood there, looking at each other in silence, while listening to the haunting echo of the army of goose calls bounce off the lake.

One of them repeated the question. "What the hell was that?"

Though they scanned the sky, they could see nothing there; and their ears acutely attuned to the night air, they could detect no motor, no jet, no sound like before — nothing but the sound of the geese settling back down.

Still disturbed by what they had witnessed, the three kept their ears open for tales of strange lights in the air that might have been witnessed by residents of the nearby communities of Levack or Onaping. But they never heard any rumblings from a town in which rumour could spread like wildfire through a drought-blanched forest, and seem to be the only ones to have heard or saw anything.

Years later, none of the three of them could ever explain what they saw that night. At times they speculated that it might have indeed been a helicopter with a search light, due to the intense light preventing them from seeing what sort of craft was hovering above them in the sky; or perhaps that it was a jet, even though they couldn't imagine a jet coming in that low over such a remote area far from any airport they were aware of.

Though his colleagues — Brian and Chummy — are now deceased, Brian Purvis occasionally mentions the eerie experience to his wife and children. It reminds him of a similar tale that his father had shared about an incident that had happened on Highway 144 in the early 1960s.

Purvis's father had shared a tale that his father's good friend Mr. Douglas had relayed to him.

* * * *

Spooky Sudbury

Douglas and his wife were driving from Cartier to Levack one quiet and lonely evening. The highway between Cartier and Levack is still a dark one, and on a moonless night, with no other cars on the road, and with your own car's headlights being the only thing cutting through the darkness, the tall trees on either side of the highway create an ominous wall, giving the illusion of driving through a canyon of curves, hills, and turns.

The couple were perhaps half-way through their journey when, from out of nowhere, a bright light appeared right behind their car.

Douglas at first thought that a car had snuck upon them without lights and suddenly flashed them on, but the light wasn't coming from directly behind them the way that a car's headlights would appear. It seemed to be coming from above them.

He pressed his foot down hard on the gas pedal, sending his car shooting down the highway, through the artificial canyon of trees on either side, trying to create some distance between his vehicle and the trailing strange light.

But the light kept coming, gaining on them, slowly closing the gap.

Worried about the high speed he was travelling, but worried more about what was pursing their car, Douglas pressed his foot right down to the floor mat, the car vibrating with the extra exertion. It seemed like an hour that the light continued to keep pace with them as their car shot dangerously down the deserted highway, but it couldn't have been more than ten minutes.

Finally, just as they were turning off of Highway 144 and onto Regional Road 8, which led to Onaping and Levack, the light disappeared.

When Purvis recalls his own experience, and the one shared by his father's friends, he wonders at the two different incidents,

The Hunter and the Hunted

their strange similarities, and if there is an explanation out there as to what, exactly was experienced both of those times.

There are no answers, only questions as one ponders the one scenario of hunters being pinned down at their campsite, and a fellow pair of residents being pursued down a dark highway — a situation in which the hunters might perhaps have, even for just a few moments, been the hunted, caught in the bright crosshairs of some undeterminable origin.

Speculative Sudbury: Bigfoot, Sasquatch, and Other Strange Creatures

"Dead Flesh Monster" by Sudbury artist Rob Sacchetto.

BIG SIGHTINGS OF LARGE-FOOTED, CRYPTID CREATURES

For hundreds of years, Native American tribes in the Pacific Northwest have shared and passed along stories concerning "wild men" living in the woods; larger-than-human, bipedal, hairy, ape-like humanoids. Versions of this type of creature exist all over the world. In Nepal, there is the Yeti; in the Himalayans, the Abominable Snowman; in places such as Russia, Mongolia, and Armenia, the creature is known as Almas.

No matter where humans are, there are similar legends of elusive creatures that keep mostly hidden from humans, even as we forge deeper into unchartered forests.

One of the most well-known documented sightings of the creature known as Bigfoot was taken by Roger Patterson and Robert Gimlin in October 1964 at Bluff Creek, California. Since that time, thousands of sightings of similar cryptid creatures have been spotted.

The vast forests of Northeastern Ontario that surround Sudbury are no stranger to sightings of a similar creature that is known as either Sasquatch or Bigfoot. Two different groups dedicated to the study, recording and analysis of such sightings

SPOOKY SUDBURY

contain multiple occurrences as reported by individuals as well as in various news reports. The groups are Ontario Bigfoot and Ontario Sasquatch. Pat Barker writes, in a post on the Ontario Sasquatch website, of the background for the different names that these human-like creatures have been given. Barker explains that "sasquatch" was a term first used by a teacher from British Columbia named John W. Burns in a 1929 *Maclean's* magazine article entitled "Introducing B.C.'s Hairy Giants." The word "sasquatch" was an anglicised version derived from the Coast Salish First Nations names for the creature— sesquac, sesxech, and suhsq'uhtch.[1]

And, while the term "sasquatch" become associated with sightings of the cryptid creatures in Canada, Barker goes on to explain how the term "bigfoot" came into popular use in the United States a little bit later. It was in 1958 that the *Humbolt Times* ran a newspaper article regarding a footprint cast seventeen inches long and six inches wide made by Jerry Crew, a member of the team working on an excavation site in Bluff Creek, California.[2] The term "bigfoot" was obviously derived from the size of the tracks left in the ground, and the name quickly fell into popular use starting then and being re-generated when the famous Patterson-Gimlin film was recorded in the fall of 1967.[3]

In December of 2012, a family filmed a video of what was believed to be the Bigfoot creature in a remote area southwest of Sudbury. A video lasting several minutes was shot; it recorded a series of the large humanoid bare footprints in the snow, in the field adjacent to the road, as well as crossing the road itself. The prints were reported as being fifteen inches long by eight inches wide and with a stride between footprints of five feet. During the video, which is posted on the Ontario Bigfoot website, you can hear the frightened and concerned voices of the children as the mother instructs the father to slow down the vehicle and of her

Big Sightings of Large-Footed, Cryptid Creatures

desire to get outside their vehicle so she can track the footprints as they disappear into the woods.[4]

In May of that year, large humanoid footprints were found in the mud near Spanish River and that same month, just north of Hanmer, a couple observed what they believed to be a sasquatch creature sitting on a log next to a swamp.[5]

A similar sighting was reported in Killarney the previous month, but this time with reported eye-contact between the creature and the observers. After a few moments of this startling encounter, the creature turned, walked away and disappeared back into the foiliage.[6]

A twelve-foot creature was spotted and photographed by cottagers in Temogami just outside their cabin in broad daylight in the spring of 2009.[7]

These are just a few of the reports as noted on the Ontario Bigfoot website.

Ontario Sasquatch has an online report database by region, and at the time of this writing shows eighty-one reports in the northwest and northeast regions of Ontario.[8]

The testimony links to an account of a witness and his girlfriend's family reporting hearing a strange sound not far from Parry Sound and Magnetawan. It was a bit after 9:00 p.m. in the evening and they heard what they at first thought were the sounds of wolves or coyotes howling. The sound, very clear, didn't sound like any coyote or wolf howls they had previously heard, and it wasn't until they listened to recordings on the Bigfoot Research Organization (BFRO) website that they wondered if it might have been the sounds of a Bigfoot creature in the nearby woods.[9]

The Temagami area, east of the Sudbury region, shows multiple reports from 2005 of witnessed incidents of broken trees, the sound of tree tapping and tracks found on an old logging road as well as two separate 1994 incidents of screams heard

SPOOKY SUDBURY

by campers at a cottage a pair of fishermen who spotted a seven-foot tall brown creature from their boat.[10]

North of the Sudbury area, in Kirkland Lake and Cobalt areas, there are seven reports going back to 1906, including the 1920s, 1940s, 1970s, 1980s, and as recent as 2006, from newspaper reported incidents in the *North Bay Nugget* of sightings, to childhood memories of seeing the strange creature doing things as benign as eating blueberries.[11]

Groups such as Ontario Bigfoot continue to do regular investigations and are staging in spots such as Blind River, the LaCloche Range south of Espanola and North of Capreol.

While the mystery of what the cryptid creatures really are and where they come from has yet to be solved, the fact is that Northeastern Ontario contains no shortage of lush rolling forested hills that will have investigators continuing to search and explore for many years to come.

THE CREATURE FROM BIG TROUT LAKE

The Sudbury area is a veritable paradise when it comes to fresh water fishing. If you leave the centre of the city and head in almost any direction, you'll find a plethora of fishing spots certain to satisfy even the most particular of avid fishermen looking for trout, perch, whitefish, bass, or walleye.

And, regardless of the many different species that may be pulled out of the nearby lakes, and of the dream of fishermen to pull a "large monster" from the depths of the water below, nobody expects to discover an actual monster hiding in the murky depths of the water. No, "a monster of a fish" is just one of many expressions that fishermen use to exaggerate their legendary catches.

But in one case, the "monster" was just that — a strange, unidentifiable creature found in the water that couldn't be explained. Although the story came from a lake quite a bit further north than the Greater Sudbury area, the tale is still fascinating for residents, particularly given the multitude of bodies of water, many of them remote and not regularly traversed or explored and which might just be hiding long-kept secrets.

SPOOKY SUDBURY

In May of 2005, a foot-long, bald-faced hairy creature with a warthog-shaped snout, long curved fangs, and a rat's tail was pulled from Big Trout Lake, a lake in remote northern Ontario.[12]

Photos and a story about the find was posted on the website of the First Nations community (Kitchenuhmaykoosib Inninuwug) and the pictures were spread online to hundreds of websites, sparking articles in newspapers and magazines across Canada and around the globe, including such headlines as "The Creature From the Deep" in the UK *Sun*.[13]

As the story goes, a pair of nurses was walking along the shoreline when their dog sniffed something in the water, then dragged a hideous, dead creature onto the shore. The two snapped the pictures which ended up being spread all over the internet.

The First Nations website also made mention of the fact that this was not the first time a creature like this has been seen. "Our ancestors used to call it the Ugly One." The website is quoted as stating: "Rarely seen but when seen, it's bad omen, something bad will happen."[14]

Speculation after the find included talk of the mythical Ogopogo or Naitaka (a Salishan term meaning "lake demon"). Ogopogo is the name commonly applied to a cryptid creature that is reported to live in Okanagan Lake in British Columbia.[15] It is a creature similar to the well-known Loch Ness Monster, and perhaps might be considered Canada's version of that famous Scottish creature, if not for other Canadian lake monsters such as Memphre, reported to live in Lake Memphremagog, Quebec,[16] Igopogo, from Lake Simcoe, Ontario,[17] or Mussie from Muskrat Lake, not far from our nation's capital.[18]

It is fascinating to discover that, while we can all see the beautiful and serene surfaces of a lake, these vast and deep bodies of water which take up so much real estate in Ontario, not to

THE CREATURE FROM BIG TROUT LAKE

mention the vast territory that is the Greater Sudbury Region, might just be holding secrets that most of us will never see.

Of course, with Mark Leslie having grown up in the home of an avid fisherman, he recalls seeing, in his father's basement workshop, an old wooden plaque with the following slogan painted onto it:

Early to bed
Early to rise
Fish like hell
And make up lies
    Fisherman's Code

Given this motto, he thinks it is a huge wonder there aren't more tales of strange creatures being pulled from the water in the region.

Strange Sudbury:
Other Oddities, Eerie Encounters, and Strangeness

BLOOD AND DARKNESS

Sometimes, when soliciting stories for a collection such as this, it works best to write the tale the way you would when crafting an article for a newspaper or magazine, occasionally quoting the interviewee and injecting background details to set the scene.

Other times, particularly when the person on the other side of the table is a writer, a crafter of words, you get so taken with the story that you forget you are interviewing them for the purposes of creating a tale.

This is that type of case.

The following story, which the author entitled "Blood and Darkness," comes from award-winning Sudbury writer and poet Melanie Marttila, who has had fiction published in the Sudbury science fiction magazine, *Parsec,* as well as poetry featured in 1998's *Neoverse* from Your Scrivener Press, 1999's *Battle Chant*, as well as *Highgrader Magazine*, and anthologies from Hidden Brook Press and Cranberry Tree Press. Melanie's Master's thesis, *Whispers in the Dark*, is a collection of short stories published by the University of Windsor Press in 1999.

SPOOKY SUDBURY

BLOOD AND DARKNESS
BY MELANIE MARTTILA

Tonsillitis is hell. The true infection, the one that leaves your four-year-old self screaming, the monster pain in your ears reaching back into your brain, your throat, latching on with needle-like claws, and shredding.

I remember that.

I don't remember the inevitable tonsillectomy, but what I do remember is what happened next.

In the middle of the night, I awoke, coughing, had trouble breathing, the air moving in and out of me with a rattling slurp, like the sound of milk bubbling through a straw. The next cough shot a black spatter onto my pyjamas and sheets. I couldn't summon the breath to call for my mom right away; my first attempt emerged as a thready burble.

Each stuttering breath and cough produced a little more noise, until I was shouting, "Mom!"

The light switch flicked on, momentarily blinding me, but one look at the blood and I yelled again, despite the jagged burning in my throat, tried to crawl back from it, but it followed. I was covered in blood.

My stitches had burst.

A frantic ride to the hospital and the doctor ordered me back into surgery and my parents were ordered out of the examination room, the male nurse assuring them that he could handle getting the intravenous inserted.

He sent Mom away. He tried to stab me. I showed him.

Mom and Dad were brought back in, allowed to hold my hand, held my legs down, while the newly bandaged nurse taped my arm to a block of wood and did his worst. In the moment, I hated them for that, for letting the nurse hurt me.

BLOOD AND DARKNESS

The road back from that second surgery was a long one. I'd ingested so much blood, I became incontinent in the most embarrassing way, my family doctor plucked clots of blood out of my ears, and nothing, not even ice cream, tasted good for weeks. I have a picture of myself right after the surgery, pale, skinny. It was Christmas, but I couldn't smile. I wore a red housecoat, huddled underneath it.

What's stayed with me the most was the dream.

My first night home, I dreamed of my bed, empty. The cheery yellow and white striped flannel sheets, the blue wool blanket turned down, the dark wood frame with the toy cupboard built in. Just the bed in a kind of spot light, the rest of the room dark. The image of the bed receded into the darkness and finally disappeared.

When I woke, I felt certain that I'd died. Calm and content, I recalled the dream, and I understood. The life I'd lived before was over. That was the dream of my sleeping self. I died in that world, and woke up in this. It made all the sense in the world.

In many ways, that's when I was born, in blood and darkness, emerging from a dream into a new life.

THE WEIRD KID:
ROB SACCHETTO

Rob Sacchetto was always "the weird kid."
Growing up in a family home on the Kingsway, next to what is now the Apollo Restaurant, he didn't have many opportunities to hang out with neighbourhood kids or other young folks around town.

Not that he would have wanted to, even if he could.

The lifelong Sudburian found his fun in the horror genre. He lived to watch monster movies, from dinosaur films to *Godzilla*. After watching a TV run of *Attack of the Mushroom People*, his interest in human/monster movies peaked.

It got to the point where he'd go to sleep after dinner so he could wake up in time for late-night movies on TV.

"My mom would say 'If you go to bed early, I'll wake you up so you can watch the movies,'" he said.

He rarely made it to the end of the second scream-inducing flick, unless it was really good.

At the same time he was watching monsters, zombies, and other creatures on TV, he was honing his artistic skills. His

THE WEIRD KID: ROB SACCHETTO

parents encouraged him, telling him that his strange creatures were great. It fuelled his desire to keep drawing.

However, being an artistic kid with a passion for monsters wasn't necessarily the best way to go about being part of the in-crowd during his youth.

"Sudbury is kind of a conservative place," he said. "Not super welcoming of weird and different things."

But it's home. While so many have been deflated by the lack of support, it just propelled Sacchetto to try harder.

"I'm from Sudbury," Sacchetto said with a laugh. "People (there) don't dig monsters. I was always an outcast, a geek ... who drew stuff."

Now that he's an adult, little has changed.

Except now he has acquired international recognition for his passion, and pays his bills by drawing weird pictures. Sacchetto's official title is "zombie portrait artist."

He creates "zombified" images of just about everything: people, celebrities, animals and beyond. He's been commissioned to create fifty-two different zombies for a deck of playing cards, he's been a named character in a graphic novel, and he's even made zombie look-alike targets for a gun company. People have his zombies tattooed on them, and he even has a daily zombie blog, where he adds another zombie portrait every day.

He's literally drawn thousands of zombies.

"I could never, ever have dreamt of my life being better than this," he said.

All because his parents encouraged his interests and he got to be that weird kid staying up late watching horror movies.

WHICH WITCH DO YOU IMAGINE WHEN SOMEONE SAYS "WITCH"?

The average person tends to think of witches each year when Halloween approaches. The witch costume, with the stereotypical black pointed hat, along with a black cat and the image of riding on a broom silhouetted by the full moon, is a popular image that most of us hold. Those who grew up watching reruns of the 1939 movie *The Wizard of Oz* might immediately envision the green-skinned evil cackling Wicked Witch of the West, as portrayed by Margaret Hamilton, rather than Glinda, the Good Witch of the South, played by Billie Burke.

Despite the more recently popular portrayal of benevolent wizards and witches in J.K. Rowling's *Harry Potter* novels, the common perception is still mostly negative. Witches, witchcraft, and Wiccan beliefs have long had negative associations. From early European witch hunts in France, Switzerland, and Germany in the fifteenth and sixteenth centuries[1] to the 1962 Salem witch trials, there simply has been no quarter given to the misunderstood and persecuted practitioners of Paganism and Wicca.

Sudbury has a few communities of practitioners of Wicca, complete with regular meetings and shops that carry gemstones,

Which Witch Do You Imagine When Someone Says "Witch"?

crystals, and Chakra pendants. The communities are often involved in a "back to nature" movement, embracing holistic, natural, or alternative medicines.

Sudbury author Dr. Chris Nash is doing what she can to at least clear the names of some of the witches who have been persecuted as a result of the outrageous mob mentality that merged ignorance, prejudice, hatred, and fear — resulting in the deaths of many innocent women.

Nash published a book in November 2012 called *Temperance Lloyd: Hanged for Witchcraft 1682*. The book explores how educated people sent three women, known as the Bideford Witches (Temperance Lloyd, Susannah Edwards, and Mary Trembles), to the gallows in England in 1682.

A psychologist by trade, Nash explores the phenomenon by which logical, reasoning individuals are blindly influenced by a hatred and fear of witchcraft and the natural healing arts. Women accused of witchcraft were declared guilty because, according to the rule of the Church, to deny witchcraft was to deny God.

Nash took creative license to fill in the gaps of these women's lives, exploring who they might have been before the tragedy befell them. "All we know," Nash says, "is that they were accused of witchcraft, tried in Exeter and hanged at Heavitree on August

Woodcut from Cotton Mathers's Wonders of the Invisible World, *1689.*

SPOOKY SUDBURY

25, 1692. This novel invites you into their lives and deaths by reading between the lines of history."[2]

The author has been vocal about a campaign launched to help absolve them of being witches and officially clear their names.

"They did nothing wrong," Nash says. "They were victims of circumstance, as were most of the people who accused them. They should be pardoned, if only as representatives of the over four hundred and fifty people who died as witches in Britain."[3]

"The story of how they came to the gallows is a tragic one that serves as a dark reminder of England's past."[4]

So, while Sudbury might not at first seem to have any direct historic witchcraft stories, it certainly has an advocate who is looking to right some of the wrongs of the past and who continues to shed light on a misunderstood and unreasonably feared practice and belief system.

THE DEFIANT EMPIRE OF BRIGITTE KINGSLEY

While most girls her age were playing with Barbie dolls or playing house, Brigitte Kingsley was watching horror movies.[5]

Kingsley, who was born in Sudbury in 1976 and grew up in Hanmer, began her on-screen career when she was still in high school, appearing in commercials for Radio Shack, Oxy, Foot Locker, and McDonald's.[6] She has long been fascinated with horror.

"There was a tree outside my window," Kingsley said in an interview with *Sudbury Star* reporter Laura Stradiotto in July of 2012. "I must have been seven years old — and I was terrified the tree would eat me because I had watched *Poltergeist*. I would sleep between the wall and my bed because I figured if the tree looked into my window, it wouldn't see me because I was against the wall."[7]

And while the horrors started in the Sudbury-area community, Kingsley is one of those souls who just couldn't leave Sudbury behind, even after her family moved away and she eventually travelled the world, pursued her dreams, and spent time in cities like Los Angeles, working with Hollywood producers.[8]

SPOOKY SUDBURY

Kingsley's hard work and perseverance led to the creation of a production company, Defiant Empire, with her husband Andrew Cymek on the aptly named Sudbury Street in Toronto, Ontario.[9]

They produced the film *Medium Raw* which was a darker retelling of the Red Riding Hood story. Kingsley says that she and her husband enjoy the horror genre, that it is fun to explore, and that certain props from their projects, such as the wolf costume with three-foot long claws from *Medium Raw* and a skull-decorated throne from the series *Dark Rising* can at times be seen on display in the couple's home.[10]

Kingsley was back in Sudbury in the summer of 2012 filming the latest in a series of *Dark Rising* projects which started with a 2006 dark humour horror flick *Dark Rising* in which she plays Summer Val, a half-human, half-demon warrior who fights demons.[11]

For the filming of *Dark Rising: Warrior of Worlds*, in early July of 2012, parts of Durham Street and Elgin Street in the city of Sudbury were shut down, for the shooting of scenes where Kingsley was racing down the street touting a massive assault weapon while hunting down a demon and being chased by monster crabs (the crabs of course, would later be added into the sequence via CGI animation).[12]

And because the plot of the storyline in *Warrior of Worlds* involves a demon-possessed nickel mine owner, the crew also shot scenes at a local mine in Copper Cliff, as well as at Science North.[13]

Kingsley expressed joy at being back in her old stomping grounds for this project, stating that her parents and best friend still live in the Greater Sudbury area.[14] And, as we have already speculated, there is something about the Nickel Capital of the world that keeps drawing people back here; something perhaps magnetic about the rich deposits of the land.

THE ENIGMA OF TOM MORLEY

In 1978 Michael Kavluk spent the summer in Levack, intent on researching and writing a brief history of his hometown. Based on a recommendation from Mayor Jim Coady and a former Levack resident, Tony Soden, and having obtained a small grant from the Ontario government to cover his room and board in one of the bunk houses, Kavluk set out for Levack.

Kavluk discovered that there were several elderly residents living in the area who remembered things "first hand" from the town's earliest days and they were happy to spend time telling him stories and sharing their photograph albums.

By the fall of 1978, Kavluk had produced a draft of the book and has continued to work on it over the years. Kavluk has always felt that the story of the history of his hometown deserved to be published; not only for the town and its history, but also out of respect for those great townspeople who shared their stories with him and supported the work.

This tale is one from his enriching and fascinating book, concerning Morley's Mine, a much talked-about man — and location — within the Levack, Onaping, and Dowling communities. Kavluk was willing to share his original tale from the still-unpublished book with readers of *Spooky Sudbury*

THE ENIGMA OF TOM MORLEY
BY MICHAEL KAVIUK

They say that he lived like a bear.

On the mountain across from High Falls, old Morley dug out a mine with no assistance and lived beside it for years in a shack made from roots and logs. He dug out a vertical shaft first. And then, when the shaft became filled with snow and rain, he dug into the side of the mountain to avoid the flooding.

He refused to allow hydro lines to be strung across his property, which he would not sell for a vast sum to the nickel companies which were eager to develop it.

And one did not just wander freely onto his property; not unless you wanted to get a close look at the old fella's weathered face while he was peering at you from the safe end of an old shotgun. Indeed, Mr. Morley liked his privacy.

It was said that he was crippled by a gunshot wound, having been mistaken for a bear while in a forest in British Columbia. Some residents of Levack remembered seeing his towering form limp into town, his walking stick digging into the earth with each weighty step.

He was a regular customer at Hughes's store, sending and receiving mail, as well as purchasing food and clothing. His supplies always included a good stock of salt pork and beans. He used to say, "What I don't taste, I won't miss."

And it was not uncommon to see him with an old tin wheelbarrow, hauling his ore all the way into Larchwood and returning with a load of dynamite. Many offered the man a ride but seldom

THE ENIGMA OF TOM MORLEY

would he accept it. If he did, he would leave ten cents on the seat behind him for their trouble. When occasionally he had to make the trip to Sudbury he would walk the long distance, stay overnight in a small hotel and return the next day, declining any offers of a ride along the way.

At Bolton's Store he would sit for hours chatting with whoever happened to drop by. In the winter a few old railway seats were set up around the large wood stove in the store, and Morley would pass the hours discussing whatever subject was current at the time. In the summer a couple of long benches outside the store were the meeting place for anyone who had the inclination to pass the time of day. He was considered a well-read man, and his thoughts and opinions were respected. The ladies remembered him well as a very polite man; a real gentleman.

Few ever got to know old Morley really well. He chose to live in seclusion. He was a religious man, and travelled to town regularly, however, to teach Sunday school to Levack's youngsters.

Ed Piaskoski was the last person to see him alive. On a chilly fall evening in 1942, Ed gave Morley a ride on his bus from Levack to his log cabin by the road at High Falls. Morley's main cabin was near his mine along a path that set out through the bush, around the hill, and up to the mine. It was dark when he let him off, and Ed offered to lend him a flashlight. Morley, however, indicated that he might stay overnight in the roadside cabin and declined the offer.

Morley was thought to be nearly eighty years old at the time. On his return trip from Sudbury Ed wondered, as he passed the roadside cabin where Morley said he might stay the night, if the old man had decided to try and find his way in the dark to his main cabin. The next day Ed's question was answered.

Tom Morley had stayed in the small cabin by the road. He died in his sleep that night with his unopened mail, unread

SPOOKY SUDBURY

newspaper, and the odd groceries that he had purchased at Hughes's Store beside him.

Sudbury Region Ghost Towns

We sometimes catch a fleeting glimpse of something that appears to be there but not there — a movement, shape, image, or even spectre — and that is typical of what a person thinks of when you use the word "ghost."

But there are other ghosts around us; ever present reminders of a time that once was, of a bustling place filled with people and places all vibrant with activity and bustle. These are once populous towns that are all but left behind in the inexorable march of progress and change.

As Ron Brown writes in his book *Ontario's Ghost Town Heritages*, these abandoned locales are "a wealth that the traveller, geographer and historian would be foolish to ignore."[15]

Ghost towns can be sad and lonely, they can sometimes carry a power and beauty that moves us; but they can also become an eerie thing for us to behold, perhaps because their existence is evidence of just how fleeting our time on this planet is.

Sudbury's relative northern locale, the booming mining history, and its juxtaposition as a railway hub connecting Southern and Eastern Ontario with North and Northeastern Ontario left it with several former "living and breathing" communities now bereft and abandoned.

Burwash, a community about forty-five miles outside Sudbury, is a good example of a locale that was built for a very specific reason. The town existed to be home for the guards and staff who worked at the Burwash Industrial Farm (aka the Burwash Correctional Centre,) which first opened in 1914. In its heyday, this provincial jail was isolated — before the construction of Highway 69 — and thus was only accessible from a nearby Canadian Northern Railway train station. It housed anywhere from one hundred and eighty to eight hundred and twenty inmates. The facility owned as much as 35,000 acres of land and leased 100,000 acres.[16]

The town, which boasted a post office, church, public school, barber shop, tailor shop, and shoe repair shop, as well as a public school and grocery store, also had a working saw mill. The trees for the mill were cut down by inmates, and the processed logs helped build the nearby village for the residents as well as picnic tables for all of Ontario's provincial parks. The inmates worked on various tasks: harvesting vegetables, making bread, and learning trades. For this reason, Burwash was considered to be an almost self-sustaining community. In the early 1970s, the prison was closed, was taken over by the military and the operation relocated elsewhere.[17, 18]

The old prison building, while deteriorating, still stands — a ghostly echo of the population that used to live within those walls.

A little closer to Sudbury, just a couple of kilometers to the north, is the ghost town of Victoria Mines. In 1899, Dr. Ludwig Mond, one of the metallurgists responsible for discovering a way to perfectly separate nickel and copper, opened the Victoria Mine townsite.[19]

The town, which was laid out on a grid of six streets, all numbered with the exception of Main Street, had both a separate

SUDBURY REGION GHOST TOWNS

and a public school, a butcher, a barber, a bowling alley, a jail, a doctor's office, and four grocery stores. The town boasted five hundred residents at one time, but before the town could really take off, nearby Coniston, which boasted better rail connections on the CPR's Sudbury-to-Toronto line, was selected a preferred site for the smelter that opened in 1913. This move signalled a death knell for the town, with company homes sawed in half and shipped off to a nearby mine at Worthington.[20]

Today, the once ambitious Victoria Mines town site, which is split almost in half by Highway 737, boasts a lone, weathered two-storey house, the last defiant soldier standing sentinel for the town that once was. Most of the formerly numbered streets are faint paths in a field, and the land where the other homes used to stand are small, almost indistinguishable depressions in the ground.[21]

A similar community, first developed by the Dominion Nickel Company (DNC) in 1889 and located just north of the city of Sudbury, was Blezard Mine. Employing upwards of three hundred people, the community consisted of a boarding house, a store, a warehouse, a school, and about twenty log homes. The mine only lasted about three years before DNC closed it down due to financial difficulties. Now, evidence of the community is all but gone, save for the old mine and the location of the smelter and roast yard sites.[22]

Much further to the north, about sixty kilometers up Highway 144, sits Benny, a town that started as a shipping point in 1880 for the Spanish, Strong, and Hope Lumber companies, under the name Pulp Siding. As it grew, the town boasted three boarding houses, a church, a poolroom, and a store, along with more than twenty cabins.[23]

In 1911, the mills shut down and things slowed down in Pulp Siding. They didn't pick up again until 1913, when the Spanish

Pulp and Paper Company started logging operations on a nearby lake. The town was re-named, from Pulp Siding to Benny, in honour of a railway engineer.[24]

As growth continued over the next dozen years, Benny had as many as seven hundred residents; a hotel, a school, and a Roman Catholic Church were built. A solitary phone line connected Benny to the outside world, and the main way in and out of town was via rail; it cost fifteen cents to take the train from Sudbury to Benny.[25]

In 1928 the mill was shut down, and, with a newly created road access, many residents moved to the nearby larger CPR station town of Cartier. By 1943, the town was a mere shadow of what it used to be, and the vacant mill burned down,[26] a sudden and dramatic statement of what its original closing meant to the community. Around that same time, the schools and grocery store were also closed down.[27]

Just a small handful of cabins still exist, within a stone's throw of the still-operational CPR rail track that runs through the town. These buildings, where a small group of residents still dwell, are the only sign of life in the town.

Even further north, and founded on the shores of Lake Biscotasi on the Spanish River in 1884 by the Canadian Pacific Railway, lies the town of Biscotasing.[28] This divisional point community was home to more than a dozen engineers and three telegraphers, Anglican and Catholic churches, a general store, a school, and boarding houses.[29]

A fiery fate similar to one that struck the mill in Benny befell this town, with a fire that raged through the town in 1912 destroying a mill and much of the town itself. It was a devastating blow, and proved to be the death knell of the town. Despite the mill and most of the town being rebuilt, it limped along for almost two decades before closing for good in 1929. By the time

Sudbury Region Ghost Towns

Ghost towns can be an eerie thing to behold, perhaps because their existence is evidence of just how fleeting our time on this planet is.

the 1920s arrived, the population had plummeted from approximately two hundred and fifty down to less than people. And even with renewed hope that came when the E.B. Eddie Company started new logging operations in the 1950s, the town's annual population hovered at a mere twenty residents.[30]

The most well-known resident of Biscotasing is someone whose existence haunts our collective Canadian psyches and whose origin are shrouded in intrigue and mystery.

A tall, hawk-nosed man emerged from the town, with an Ojibwa name, Wa-sha-quon-asin, which translated to "great grey owl." Chief Grey Owl, as he became known to the general public, rose to prominence as a notable lecturer, writer, and "apostle" of the wilderness.[31]

The author of such books as *The Men of the Last Frontier* (1931), *Pilgrims of the Wild* (1934), and *Tales of an Empty Cabin*

SPOOKY SUDBURY

(1936),[32] Grey Owl was a nature and conservation advocate and has often been credited with being responsible for saving the Canadian beaver from extinction.[33]

It wasn't until the time of his death, in 1938, that newspapers such as the *North Bay Nugget* exposed the fact that this renowned Indian was not an Indian at all, but a British-born man by the name of Archibald Belaney who had moved to Biscotasing in 1912.[34]

Despite the ruse by which he had fooled everyone, Grey Owl made a distinct impression on conservation movements. Several films and books have been produced about the legacy he left behind, and his viewpoints regarding the necessity for a respect for nature continue to be held in the highest of regard.

Surely this is evidence of the power that ghosts and ghost towns can have long after they are no longer a part of our living and breathing world.

UNDERGROUND GHOST HUNTERS AND THE SEARCH FOR DARK MATTER

In his book *Great Northern Ontario Mines*, author Michael Barnes looks at a unique technological innovation associated within the hundred-year-old Creighton Mine in a chapter entitled "Ghost Hunters Underground."[35]

Barnes isn't, of course, talking about spirits of the dead, but rather neutrinos — the sub-atomic building block particles for the universe that originate in the centre of the sun and are the product of exploding stars. Barnes states that "they are ghosts or phantoms because although theorists tell us that one hundred billion neutrinos pass through an area the size of a fingertip every second at the speed of light, they are very difficult to detect."[36]

These tiny ghost-like neutrinos, Barnes writes, which pass through everything at virtually undetectable speeds, are not stopped by the two kilometres (6800 feet) of rock which do filter out the bombardment of cosmic rays. That, combined with the Creighton Mine area site exuding an extremely low level of natural radiation, gave the least possible interference with the required scientific observations.[37]

Spooky Sudbury

The Sudbury Neutrino Observatory (SNO) is part of what is now known of as SNOLAB, an underground science laboratory located two kilometers below the surface at the Vale/Inco Creighton Mine, created as part of a project proposed by Laurentian University, Carleton University, Queen's University, the University of British Columbia, the University of Guelph, and the Université de Montréal.[38]

And while the principle focus of SNOLAB continues to be particle astrophysics, the enhanced lab, which includes a large surface building at Creighton Mine, as well as a facility for radio-isotope measures and water analysis at nearby Laurentian University, supports growing interest from related fields, such as Seismology, Geophysics, and Biology.[39]

Laurentian University and SNO feature prominently in international bestselling science fiction author Robert J. Sawyer's novels. Sawyer, who lives in Mississauga, Ontario, spent some time in Sudbury when doing research for his Hugo Award-winning book *The Neanderthal Parallax* trilogy, which includes the books *Hominids*, *Humans* and *Hybrids*. Sawyer used the setting as the premise for a quantum computer event that creates a portal between two parallel worlds — one in which humans, descendants of Cro-Magnons, people the world, and the other by descendants of the Neanderthals.

As part of his research, Sawyer spent time with scientists and researchers at Laurentian University and the SNO and went down the two kilometres to explore and understand it, in order to create a realistic setting for his award-winning novels. And, while Sawyer's novels, — based on existing science, research, and studies, combined with that unique speculative "what if" element of good science fiction — are fiction, they illustrate the wonder and intrigue involved in exploring more about the underlying building blocks of the universe that we live in that

UNDERGROUND GHOST HUNTERS AND THE SEARCH FOR DARK MATTER

are taking place every day right under the feet of Sudburians.

The trip down to the heart of SNO takes approximately sixty-five minutes in an elevator that is approximately half the size of a single-car garage,[40] and eventually leads to the SNO detector. The detector is situated in the SNO cavern, is thirty metres tall and twenty metres across; it is the largest cavern at this depth in the world. The SNO detector uses 1,000 tonnes of heavy water contained in an acrylic vessel that is 12 metres in diameter 5 centimetres thick and bonded together using 122 separate panels polished to optical quality. There are 9600 Photomultiplier Tubes mounted in a geodesic sphere 18.4 metres in diameter surround the acrylic vessel are used to detect the interactions of neutrinos in the heavy water.[41]

Physicists are fascinated with neutrinos and studying them in this facility because the otherwise undetectable visitors reach the earth from the sun in mere minutes compared with the thousands of years it takes other particles to reach the earth from the same distance.[42] Studying these unseen particles helps these scientists understand how our universe works and can inform the detection of supernovas (the explosive and spectacular death of a massive star).[43]

Astronomers and astrophysicists have also come to determine that as much of 25 percent of matter in the universe is made out of a non-luminous cosmological matter known as "Dark Matter." This dark matter, which was once thought to be neutrinos, is fundamental to our understanding of the structure and the evolution of galaxies, due to the nature by which it interacts with gravity, serving to shape and hold together galaxies and clusters of galaxies.[44]

So the next time you are standing in a room, alone, and get the feeling that there is something else there, it might not be the standard ghost.

SPOOKY SUDBURY

If you ever see the shimmering spectre of a humanoid figure out of the corner of your eye and you shake your head and wonder if you are imagining things, take heed: based on the ground-breaking research happening a couple of kilometers under the surface of the Greater City of Sudbury, there is indeed *something* that is always there, whether visitors from a nearby alien star or "Dark Matter" that helps make up everything, including you.

NORTHERN ONTARIO'S LORD OF GORE: PETER MIHAICHUK

A visual artist who focuses on exploring the darker side of the human psyche, Peter Mihaichuk's talent and aptitude has led him to a successful career in both television and film.[45]

Born and raised in Sudbury, Peter returned fourteen years after leaving for the Toronto area in order to raise his family in his beloved home town. With over a decade of experience in the art, sets, props, and MUFX departments of various projects in both Canada and the U.S., his big break came when he was showing his work at the Hyena Gallery in California, which took place at the same time as a nearby horror convention.[46]

Peter's dynamic exhibit became the "official stopover" between the horror event and within just a couple of hours nearly 1,500 people, including film industry professionals, saw his work. It was shortly after this serendipitous event that he was approached to do concept work for horror films and began to develop a reputation as "Northern Ontario's Lord of Gore."[47]

His eclectic background of industrial design combined with the fine arts has served him well in his role in the film industry,

SPOOKY SUDBURY

particularly since it requires a combination of both aesthetics and functionality.

Although Mihaichuk does work on non-horror projects, such as television's *The Kennedys* mini-series (2011), he regularly returns to the darker artistic projects for shows like *Falling Skies* (2011) and the movies *A Little Bit Zombie* (2012) and *Dark Rising: Warrior of Worlds* (2013).

A Little Bit Zombie, for which Peter was the production designer, was filmed in Sudbury. One of the many tasks that he had required sketching out how the main character would slowly transform into a zombie and then giving those drawings to the makeup artist for the next step. Casey Walker, director of the film, left a lot of room for Peter to insert his own creative expression.[48]

"There was a lot of me in that movie," Mihaichuk said in an interview with *Sudbury Star* reporter Laura Stradiotto in a July 2012 interview. And though he admitted to being well-acquainted with zombies and the subject matter associated with dark films, Mihaichuk admits he was never a horror buff, and that his work was just "emotionally dark."[49]

When he was a student, he mused, he often got into trouble for doodling; his grade two teacher contacted social services after he painted a tornado complete with severed body parts caught within the raging storm.[50]

While the Lasalle Secondary School graduate has had the pleasure of working on all types of films and in many different locales in North America, he told the *Northern Life* in a May 2011 interview with Jenny Jelen that he particularly enjoys working on northern productions. Working on projects close to his wife and two children is particularly appealing to this family man.[51]

"I try to take the northern work as much as possible," he said during the interview. "The opportunities to stay home and work are fortunately increasing."[52]

Northern Ontario's Lord of Gore: Peter Mihaichuk

In that same interview, Mihaichuk noted that Greater Sudbury's "central" northern location and geographic diversity make it an ideal setting for film productions; that the city has everything that makes up a "blue-collar town," as well as "upper-end neighbourhoods," to appeal to a number of different production needs.[53]

Mihaichuk says that some of the world's leading horror writers and directors had blue-collar upbringings: Wes Craven (*Nightmare on Elm Street*) grew up in Cleveland, Ohio, and author Stephen King was born in Portland, Maine.[54]

"A lot of us are from blue-collar backgrounds," Mihaichuk, whose grandfather was a miner and whose father worked in the smelter, told the *Sudbury Star*. "I'm not sure where that dynamic comes in, other than a heavy industrial background. It does lend itself a bit to the appeal of the genre … in my case, I'm known for the gritty look I bring to film."[55]

And though he likes working close to home and to his family, he says that the details of his work aren't something that he care share with his children. "A lot of times they want to see this stuff, but they can't," he says, "It's rated beyond them."[56]

And while the work on movies might be seen by some as glamorous, Mihaichuk explains that the work days can be long and demanding, often totalling as much as seventeen hours in the heart of a production, followed consecutively by similarly long days.[57] It is a good thing, then, that he is able to do something he is so passionate about.

THE DONNELLYS' TOMBSTONE

The Donnelly family, or "The Black Donnellys" as they are also referred, are a well-known part of Canadian folklore, particularly since the 1954 publication of Thomas Kelley's book *The Black Donnellys*. Kelley presented the first book, which was published by Harlequin, as being based on events leading up to the vigilante committee massacre of five family members on February 4, 1880, in Biddulph Township, Ontario. He followed it with the fictional *Vengeance of the Black Donnellys* (the story of Johannah Donnelly's supposed uttered curse that every one of her killers would die a violent death) less than ten years later.[58]

Although Kelley's first book about the family is one of the best known, and credited with bringing the Donnelly story to mass attention, it is said in a review on the Official Donnelly Home Page that although it's the most famous book on the massacre, it is not considered historically accurate.[59]

Interestingly, Kelley, who was born in Campbellford, Ontario, began his writing career composing pulp stories for such magazines as *Weird Tales* and *Uncanny Tales*.[60] It seems like, when

THE DONNELLYS' TOMBSTONE

presented with a tragic historic tale, Kelley couldn't resist embellishing the true-crime narrative into a more suspenseful and pulp-like tale for the masses.

The Donnelly gravestone, which was erected in 1963 by descendants of the family "did not mince words," as Orlo Miller states in his book *The Donnellys Must Die*. The gravestone records that John, James, Johannah, Thomas, and Bridget were "murdered."[61]

But it is curious to see how one of Canada's most infamous legends of murder has a connection to the Sudbury area.

Over the decades, multiple rumours spread over what happened with the original tombstone, the one erected in 1889 by William Donnelly and which was the subject of vandalism. The FAQ section of the Official Donnelly Home Page says that "like Elvis, it has been spotted all over Ontario, from St. Catherines to Sudbury," and that others believe it might very well be buried underneath decades of cobwebs in the basement of St. Patrick's Roman Catholic Church on the Roman Line.[62]

It was revealed, on this same website, that the original tombstone ended up in Levack, Ontario, brought there by William and Nora Donnelly's grandson and granddaughter, who placed it in their garage in two pieces. The Levack-area resident and descendent did not wish to be associated with the famous Lucan-area family, and respectfully requested that their name not be published on the website.[63]

Further investigation with townspeople of Levack revealed a family heirloom ring owned by a still living descendent, as well as a secretive manoeuvre in the middle of the night to retrieve and store the tombstone. But again, out of respect for the family's privacy, the names were withheld.

The tombstone, a much-sought-after relic of Canadian history sits somewhere in storage, in either a basement or garage

SPOOKY SUDBURY

just a forty minute drive outside of Sudbury — another mystery associated with this infamous family that lies right here in our own backyard.

THE OLD HAG HELD ME DOWN WHILE ALIENS ABDUCTED MY GOD HELMET!

Ghost stories transcend culture, history, class, and racial groups. Belief in the supernatural is one thing that most groups, tribes, or cultures have in common; ghosts or the notion of transcendence are considered culturally universal and stem back to ancient religious views such as animism (the attribution of a living soul to natural objects such as plants and animals as well as inanimate objects, or the belief in a supernatural power that organizes and animates the universe)[64] and veneration of the dead.

Spiritual interpretations of ghosts are seen in classic literature such as Homer's *The Odyssey* and Virgil's *The Aeneid*, and Shakespeare's *Hamlet*, as well as the Old and New Testaments, and endure into modern times.[65]

Studying or scientifically documenting ghosts has historically been met with great challenges, due to the individual manner by which this phenomenon is typically experienced, as well as the fact that researchers typically only have "ghost experiences" rather than actual ghosts to study. The earliest attempts by science to study ghosts, made in the nineteenth century, weren't concerned with whether or not ghosts exist, but rather with a

SPOOKY SUDBURY

question, posed in 1942 by researcher GNM Tyrrell: "Do people experience apparitions?"[66]

The answer to Tyrrell's question, something that has fascinated physical and paranormal researchers for ages, leads to our own back yard. Indeed, research into a potential cause for this type of sensation might just exist right here in Sudbury at Laurentian University.

Born on June 26, 1945, in Jacksonville, Florida, Dr. Michael Persinger has published more than two hundred technical articles and has been a professor at Laurentian University since 1971, where he organized the Behavioral Neuroscience Program, one of the first to integrate Chemistry, Biology, and Psychology. Dr. Persinger's primary goal was to discern the commonalities that exist between the sciences, coupled with the assumption that the human brain and its microstructure are the source of all human knowledge.[67]

Dr. Persinger was intrigued by the illusionary explanations for human consciousness. Specifically, he studied the manner by which applying complex electromagnetic fields to discern the patterns (of human consciousness) would induce experiences that were often attributed to the sensed presences that range from aliens to gods.[68] According to Dr. Persinger, two thousand years of philosophy have taught us that attempting to prove — or disprove — realities may never have distinct verbal (linguistic) solutions because of the limitation of this measurement.[69] But he also stated in the episode "God on the Brain" from BBC *Horizons* that "feeling something beyond yourself, bigger in space and time, can be stimulated."

In experiments at Laurentian University, Persinger has been able to stimulate the temporal lobes of the limbic system of subjects using a yellow Ski-Doo helmet wired with a series of wires and electrodes, which the media has taken to calling the "God

THE OLD HAG HELD ME DOWN WHILE
ALIENS ABDUCTED MY GOD HELMET!

Helmet." The helmet, designed by Persinger and Stanley Koren, emits weak fluctuating electromagnetic fields approximately as strong as a telephone headset or a standard hair dryer.[70]

Although no two people seem to respond in exactly the same way to the electrical stimulus, all the individuals tested have emerged with a profound sense that something extraordinarily significant has taken place before them.

For the experiments, subjects are seated in a relaxed position in a reclining chair in a dark, mostly sensory deprived room, with blinders placed over their eyes to remove visual sensory stimulation and the aforementioned helmet on their head.

Subjects in the experiment encounter everything from cartoon characters and dead relatives, to the feeling of being kidnapped by aliens. Persinger has found a correlation between those who report the "alien encounter and kidnapping" feelings and seismic activities.[71]

Wired magazine reporter Jack Hitt wrote about his personal experiences in Dr. Persinger's lab and, though he was mostly underwhelmed by the events that took place, relative to the "great expectations and anxieties" he had going in, he did admit to having a distinct sense of being withdrawn "from the envelope" of his body and set adrift on what he called "an infinite existential emptiness, a deep sensation of waking slumber."[72]

Hitt's experiences, which skewed toward happier and pleasant memories from his youth — even events and details he had not thought about or remembered for years — are just one type of response, and perhaps one of the less disturbing side effects of the stimulating electrical inputs. But not all experiences fall into the "pleasant daydream" state. Reactions are as different as the people involved, with results that range from awe-inspiring to bizarre, from interesting illusions to outright terrifying encounters.[73]

Spooky Sudbury

As Dr. Persinger has explained, the right hemisphere, typically concerned with the "fight or flight" response and similar survival mechanisms of our brain, can trigger threatening or ominous fear-inspiring events, such as a powerful and terrifying presence, often attributed to aliens or ghosts. On the other hand, stimulation of the left side of the brain, the side most often associated with communication and language, is typically associated with reports from subjects of hearing voices, perhaps otherworldly voices and instructions, some of which could be interpreted as being the voice of God or of angels.[74]

Perhaps in the same way that Yoda explains to Luke in the classic George Lucas film *The Empire Strikes Back* when the young Jedi is sent into the dark forest and, against his master's warning, brings his light saber (which ends up being used against him). Subjects bring their own experiences, beliefs, and

The Nightmare *(oil on canvas)*, Johann Heinrich Füssli, 1781.

fears in to the experiment, helping to pepper the results with their own biases, preferences, and interpretations.

Some of the subjects of the experiments described distorted faces, voices, and bright lights and that the fear they felt was like "the closest I've ever been to hell." Conversely, others expressed a feeling of something watching them over their shoulder, but they remained peace with the presence.[75]

"What we have found," Dr. Persinger says, "is that individuals who show a temporal lobe sensitivity or creativity and who are very religious, in that setting will have a religious experience."[76]

A British psychology professor, Dr. Susan Blackmore, who underwent the procedure for the BBC *Horizons* episode "God on the Brain," later wrote about her experiences for *New Scientist* magazine. In her description, she expressed feeling sudden waves of emotion such as anger and fear, as well as a bizarre hallucinatory experience, similar to having two hands grabbing her shoulders and bodily yanking her upright. She went on to describe the feeling of something grabbing onto her leg and pulling it, distorting it and dragging it up a wall. "I knew I was still lying in the reclining chair," she wrote, "but something or someone was pulling me up."[77, 78]

Later on, Blackmore wrote about the nearly four million Americans who claim to have been abducted by aliens and considered the theory of sleep paralysis to explain it. Sleep paralysis is the sensation that some people have when they wake up of being unable to move or speak, often while sensing a powerful presence in the room, seeing lights, or hearing an odd buzzing noise. This sensation is sometimes accompanied by the feeling of a visible or invisible entity sitting on a person's chest.[79]

The presence that people often sense during these moments can be vague and indefinable but are regularly characterized as inciting intense fear, or with a feeling of a menacing evil.

Spooky Sudbury

Combined with the sudden rush of anxiety and reports of difficulty in breathing (often accompanying reports of pressure on the person's chest), it is interesting to note how closely this lies with reports of the visits by the nightmare spirit or the old hag legends of English and Newfoundland folklore.[80]

As David J. Hufford writes in his book *The Terror That Comes in the Night*, the "Old Hag" is well known to most Newfoundlanders in such a way that it is not uncommon to hear someone say "I was hagged last night." Stories involving the hag include awakening while lying on their back and either being strangled or having the hag sit on their chest so that they couldn't breathe.[81]

The phenomenon of sleep paralysis is something that tends to begin in adolescence, with some people continuing to experience the phenomenon regularly throughout their lives. Scientists propose that sleep paralysis is an "anomalous form" of the state of REM sleep, the state in which most dreams are experienced. According to their theories, the biological mechanism that prevents the body from acting out one's dreams, keeping a person, in a sense, paralysed so they can safely sleep and dream, sometimes lingers for a few moments upon awakening, bringing about the sensations described here.[82]

But regardless of whether this fascinating experience that can either impress or terrify the subjects is a result of a biological sleep side-effect or a low level electrical or seismic stimulation of the brain (or perhaps even a combination of the two), it does not dispute the manner by which it can affect people.

Logic, reasoning, and deductive thought are not at all at the forefront when we wake suddenly in the middle of the night. And the next time you wake with the sensation that you are paralysed and there is someone or something present in the room with you, something powerful and ominous, how likely are you to remember Dr. Persinger's study or the details from a psychology textbook?

The Old Hag Held Me Down While Aliens Abducted My God Helmet!

Us neither. We'll likely scream bloody hell, struggle desperately to escape the aliens standing at our bedside and looking down at us or perhaps seek a ritual to defeat the old hag who slips into our room in the middle of the night.

You know, just to be safe.

Spooky Resources:

Useful and Interesting Resources for Further Reading and Exploration of the Sudbury Region

Pulling together this book involved a variety of research and interview methods. People submitted their stories to us via email and web form, we spoke to them on phone, they met us in coffee shops, restaurants and malls, or we went to see them in their offices, homes, and workplaces. We also spent hours poring through texts, newspaper archives, and websites.

When writing about a place and its people, particularly one as dynamic as Greater Sudbury, one of the most wonderful pleasures is the discovery of just how robust and fascinating a place is. Research, of course, also involved reading and learning about elements that aren't necessarily central to Sudbury but which seem to bisect the community's historical or cultural path.

This section of the book, then, is our attempt to draw together a list of some of the resources we consulted or visited which we were either able to gather information from or simply found useful, interesting, and worth sharing with readers of this book.

SPOOKY SUDBURY

PLACES

One of the most satisfying things to do when you are putting together a non-fiction book has to do with the personal encounters involved. Places to go and people to speak to seemed without limit in Sudbury and we thought it would be useful, both for those who live in the region to be that much more aware of the great resources that exist within their home town, and for those who do not live in Sudbury but are interested in learning just a bit more about all that there is to discover and do in a town that is rich with so many different aspects.

Bell Mansion and Bell Park

Built in 1907, the Bell Mansion was commissioned by lumber baron William Joseph Bell and constructed using cut local stone. From the website:

"The original Bell Mansion property encompassed 155 acres adjacent to Lake Ramsey. Three of the original buildings on the home site remain today; the mansion; the coach house, originally detached; and a stone out-building on John Street, originally used for storage and laundry facilities ... Mr. and Mrs. Bell took great pride in the landscaping and gardens and employed a gardener throughout their residency. Stone walls defined the gradual slope to the lake. The original vegetable gardens were at the lower level on the site of 483 Elizabeth Street. Pathways were covered in white stone."

Bell bequeathed his entire estate to the people of Sudbury, to remain as a park. The Bell Mansion houses the Art Gallery of Sudbury today and the land remains a beautiful park on the shores of Lake Ramsey, with many facilities for our citizens to enjoy.

Website: www.artsudbury.org

RESOURCES

The Big Nickel (Dynamic Earth)

Home to the Big Nickel, Dynamic Earth, one of Science North's interactive science museums, was created in 2003 and is built upon the city's rich mining heritage and focuses on geology and mining-related exhibits.

The idea for the Big Nickel was born in 1963 from a contest sponsored by the Sudbury Canada Centennial Committee, requesting Sudbury citizens to provide suggestions on how they would like to see the City of Sudbury celebrate the Canadian Centennial. Ted Szilva, a 28-year-old fireman, put forward the idea of a giant replica of a nickel at the site of an underground mine and science centre. Despite Szilva's idea being rejected, he believed it to be a viable project and so purchased land between Sudbury and Copper Cliff near Regional Road 55 and what became known as Big Nickel Drive. On July 27, 1964, the Big Nickel attraction/park was officially opened, showcasing a thirty foot tall 1951 replica of the twelve-sized coin which has become synonymous with the city of Sudbury and its nickel heritage.

Website: www.sciencenorth.ca/dynamic-earth

Cambrian College

From the website:

"Cambrian College in Sudbury, Ontario, has been a leading postsecondary institution in Northern Ontario since its first classes were held in 1967. The College has a vibrant community of more than 14,000 learners — over 4,500 students in 70 full-time programs, plus over 7,500 students in almost 900 part-time courses/programs. It offers programming at three campuses and serves a student population that is reflective of the rich diversity of today's global workplaces."

Website: www.cambriancollege.ca

SPOOKY SUDBURY

Collège Boréal

From the website:

"Founded in 1995, Collège Boréal is the only French-language community college in northern Ontario. It has also served central and south-western Ontario since 2002. Collège Boréal exists to increase access to public post-secondary education for the francophone population. In September 2009, we inaugurated a new campus in Timmins and started construction of a second student residence."

Website: www.collegeboreal.ca

Laurentian University

From the website:

"Often referred to as the 'academic resort of Ontario', Laurentian University is nestled into a pristine 765-acre peninsula in Sudbury. Laurentian University is a large, diverse and highly decentralized organization comprised of four federated universities, five faculties, and several research institutes, along with many supporting administrative departments, each managed individually ... The quality of research at Laurentian has shown impressive growth, twice capturing the #1 rank for research income growth among primarily undergraduate universities by Research InfoSource. This research excellence, combined with engaging teaching styles make for the perfect learning environment."

Website: www.laurentian.ca

Rainbow Country Travel Association (RCTA) / Sudbury Welcome Centre

During his final two years of high school and his first year of post-secondary education, Mark Leslie worked for the Rainbow

Resources

Country Travel Association. He divided his time between the booth in the Dowling location (now re-located to High Falls, several kilometres further northwest on Highway 144) as well as at the RCTA location at the Sudbury Welcome Centre on Highway 69 and Whippoorwill Road. Mark experienced first-hand all of the valuable and exciting information that this association provides to both residents as well as tourists who are looking to discover all of the richness that the Sudbury region has to offer.

Website: www.rainbowcountry.com

Science North

From the website:

"Science North is Northern Ontario's most popular tourist attraction and an educational resource for children and adults across the province. Science North maintains the second- and eighth-largest science centres in Canada: (1) Science North — featuring an IMAX® theatre, digital Planetarium, butterfly gallery and Special Exhibits Hall, and (2) Dynamic Earth — Home of the Big Nickel, an earth sciences centre.

In addition to the two science centres in Sudbury, Science North also oversees an award-winning Large Format Film production unit and an Exhibit Sales and Service unit, which develops custom and ready-made exhibits for sale or lease to science centres, museums, and other cultural institutions all over the world.

Science North, in partnership with Laurentian University, have developed North America's first and only comprehensive Science Communication program, a ten-month joint graduate diploma program."

Website: www.sciencenorth.ca

SPOOKY SUDBURY

The Sudbury Library

From the website:

"The Greater Sudbury Public Library strives to enrich the lives of individuals and the spirits of the community by providing the highest quality of services to our citizens in their quest to read, learn, educate and dream. Offering over 13 locations in Greater Sudbury, the library supports all members of the community by providing equitable access to a wide variety of literature and information sources ... The library's main downtown location houses the Mary C. Shantz Room on the lower research level, a room dedicated to local history and which contains archives of local newspapers and magazines, along with census records, photographs, pamphlets, and church, cemetery, and funeral home records." Important research for *Spooky Sudbury* took place thanks to the assistance and support of Sudbury library staff members and services.

Website: www.sudburylibraries.ca

Sudbury Theatre Centre

Officially incorporated in 1971, the Sudbury Theatre Centre (STC) staged plays in the Fraser Auditorium at Laurentian University as well as at Cambrian College and the Inco Club, just a year after Sonja Dunn, Carolyn Fouriezos, Bill Hart, Bob Remnant, and Peg Roberts helped bring the Gryphon Theatre Company of Barrie's extremely successful (both financially and artistically) production of Neil Simon's *Come Blow Your Horn* to town. In 1980, the city of Sudbury donated a segment of municipal land to the STC so that they could have their very own permanent home on Shaughnessy Street. Besides putting on an ongoing series of successful shows, STC also teaches youth drama classes, produces study guides to accompany their stage

RESOURCES

productions and has been a vibrant part of Sudbury's artistic community for more than four decades.

Website: www.sudburytheatre.on.ca

WEBSITES AND OTHER ONLINE RESOURCES

Though websites are always subject to change and active web links can't be assured on a permanent basis, here are a few of the sites that we stumbled upon (along with their present site addresses)which we were either able to gather information from for the purposes of references used in this book, or we at least found their content interesting and intriguing and worth sharing with readers of *Spooky Sudbury*.

Night Fright Show

Hosted by Brent Holland, *Night Fright Show*, whose slogan is "your voice in the dark for paranormal and conspiracy" is a video/podcast/radio show that began in 2008 and was broadcast live late at night from the CKLU studios at Laurentian University, which were located on the third floor of the Parker Building on the Laurentian University Campus. Within six months of its start, the show was syndicated on eighty different stations.

Spooky Sudbury co-author Mark Leslie had the pleasure of being in the studio on two separate occasions in 2010 and can attest to the fact that, being in such an isolated location on an already isolated campus late at night, talking about creepy things that go bump in the night can certainly be an unsettling experience. Look on the Night Fright website for archives mentioning Leslie's books *Campus Chills* (2010) and *Haunted Hamilton* (2013).

233

Spooky Sudbury

Although Holland moved away from Sudbury and the radio program retired, he continues his eerie "night fright" talk show in a video format, available online via YouTube as well as broadcast weekly on TVCOGECO across Ontario.

Website: www.nightfrightshow.com

YouTube link: www.youtube.com/user/nightfrightshow

Northern Ontario UFO Research & Study (NOUFORS)

From the website:

"Since 2007, Michel M. Deschamps has worked on creating a website originally based on the research performed using the newspaper archive at Laurentian University. NOUFORS has expanded to include a wide range of ufological information gathered from international sources — everything from Sightings made by Astronauts and Police officers to Physical Trace Evidence left behind by landed objects of unknown origin. Deschamps presents the hard facts to the best of his abilities, and encourages the reader to look at the material with an open mind, and perhaps learn something new and fascinating, along the way.

Deschamps continues to inform the public about UFOs and Flying Saucers by lecturing on the subject and articles he has written which have appeared in *The Canadian Ufologist*, a Mutual UFO Network (MUFON) Ontario newsletter. His expertise lies in researching Northern Ontario newspaper archives for UFO reports and UFO-related information. Apart from those retrieved from the *Sudbury Star*, both he and his colleague Todd Fraser have located hundreds of news clippings within the pages of the *Sault Star*, the *Timmins Daily Press*, the *Kirkland Lake Northern Daily News*, and the *North Bay Nugget*.

Since July 1974, Deschamps has had just under thirty separate UFO sightings, including two captured on video and he has

Resources

appeared on numerous radio and television programs including *Midday Q, In the North, MCTV Today, Volt* (TFO) and *The Camilla Scott Show* (CTV).

Deschamp's website contains an extensive list of articles, audio, and video clips from his appearances and various eyewitness testimony, is dedicated to all those eyewitnesses, past and present, who dared to speak out but were never heard."

Website: www.noufors.com

The Official Donnelly Home Page

The Official Donnelly Home Page allows people to discover and explore one of Canada's most notorious families who were massacred February 4th, 1880 by a vigilante committee. Although parts of the website are graphic in nature, the intent of the website is not to glorify elements of the Donnelly massacre, but rather inform and educate the public on the history of the family, the town and the tragedy.

With over 750,000 visitors since its inception in May 1997, this website offers the curious virtually everything they need to know about the Donnellys, from historical, genealogical and tourism information to family photographs, updated research and even a Donnelly ghost page.

Website: www.donnellys.com

Ontario Abandoned Places

Featuring over 90,000 photographs that cover more than 4,000 abandoned sites in Canada, this website is free to use. Basic members can freely browse and discover all publicly posted locations. Full Membership allows access to more than 1100 additional locations that are not visible with a basic membership — full membership is not something that can be paid for,

SPOOKY SUDBURY

but, instead, earned by active members who contribute photos, history and stories to the website.

Website: http://www.ontarioabandonedplaces.com

Ontario Bigfoot

From the website:

"Ontario Wildlife Field Research-Ontario Bigfoot (OWFR-OB) is made up of volunteer outdoor enthusiasts, researchers and investigators who all demonstrate a love of the great outdoors and the wildlife in it. Members range from Photographers and videographers to audio specialists and trackers, all pursuing a mission of is to explore, understand and document the nature and prevalence of known and unknown wildlife in Ontario, Canada.

OWFR-OB's researchers and investigators are keenly interested in the unexplained and solving mysteries. From known to the unknown wildlife found in Ontario. OWFR-OB strives for a better understanding of the true diversity found in the deep Ontario woods. It's stranger than you might think. OWFR-OB regularly heads into the Ontario bush on expeditions to research and investigate wildlife. OWFR-OB believes in order to reach our goal in terms of research we need to be out there as much as possible. Plus we have a great time.

We believe we are unique because of a few things. Such as we are open and genuinely interested with what others have to say. Unlike most research groups we are not a closed and secretive group. Other than keeping names and exact locations confidential we make an extra effort to share what we know and experience. We are not self appointed experts, although we do have individual interests that we continually try to build and learn more about and share with the members and the public alike. We believe that we are all a team and no individual is more

RESOURCES

important than the rest. Every member in OWFR-OB is welcome and appreciated. We are all serious researchers and are all interested in solving wildlife mysteries and helping understand what would benefit all wildlife in Ontario. Our group is firmly committed to shaping the policies that govern preservation, protection and research of any and all wildlife in Ontario especially endangered species."

Website: http://ontariobigfoot.com

Ontario Sasquatch

From the website:

"Formed in 2006 with five founding members, Ontario Sasquatch (OS) is a private, non-profit organization made up of independent researchers who are investigating the existence of Sasquatch or bigfoot in Ontario. OS believes Sasquatch exists and is a flesh and blood hominid that is well adapted to its habitat.

In February of 2007, Ontario Sasquatch got our website up and running; since then, our membership has grown considerably and now includes team members in most areas of the province.

Each investigator volunteers their time without funding from outside sources. We are a group of people who are curious about the many eye witness sightings that occur across our province. Something must be happening. However, we are also skeptical.

As members of the OS team, we benefit from working with a group of people who share the same enthusiasm and interest in this subject. It's a climate in which we're able to trade experiences, gain expertise and learn from each other, one where co-operation and camaraderie is very important … We make all efforts to conduct our field work in a professional and scientific manner. This can take time. We may contact a witness many times to get all the information necessary to complete a report. If it's warranted,

SPOOKY SUDBURY

we will visit the site of the encounter. We may ask the witness to accompany us to the area. Field notes, measurements, and photos will be taken. Protocols are important, particularly when it involves collecting physical evidence, like tissue, hair and fecal samples, casting tracks, and documenting evidence in the field.

We understand that when a person sees something that isn't supposed to exist it can be a life-changing experience. Not only is there a shock factor involved, but there is often ridicule and disbelief from family and friends if they talk about their experience. We're here to help those who contact us. We will listen and do our best to look into the encounter."

Website: http://www.ontariosasquatch.com

ParaNorthern

From the website:

"'Paranormal' is a general term (coined ca. 1915–1920) that designates experiences that lie outside 'the range' of normal experience or scientific explanation or that indicates phenomena understood to be outside of science's current ability to explain or measure." - Wikipedia

Many people have a story, strange image in a photo or even a video clip of something they cannot explain. Many more people want to hear your stories.ParaNorthern.ca is a place for you to share your stories."

Website: www.paranorthern.ca

Rob Sacchetto's Zombie Portraits

If you are a zombie fan then you must have a zombie portrait, and why not from a Sudbury area artist who has been doing this since 2006, because he has always been a zombie fan, and not just riding the recent wave of popularity that zombies have taken recently.

RESOURCES

A zombie portrait is a custom hand-illustrated and painted portrait depicting the subject as a brain-eating zombie. These are hand-illustrated and painted portraits created by renowned horror artist Rob Sachetto based on a supplied photo. Turn your photo into a zombie portrait today!

Zombie Portrait artist Rob Sacchetto is a twenty-five-year veteran freelance artist and he has been illustrating custom zombie portraits full-time since 2006. He was the first artist to offer a custom zombie portrait service and his commissions remain the most sought after. In fact, Sacchetto was commissioned to create a zombie portrait for Greg Nicotero; the co-executive producer, director and special effects make-up designer on AMC's *The Walking Dead*. In addition, the staff of *The Talking Dead* also recently commissioned Rob to create a custom zombie portrait for show host Chris Hardwick.

Rob's work as appeared in *Stuff Magazine*, *Rue Morgue*, *Fangoria*, *Maxim*, *HorrorHound*, *National Geographic* and more. His work has also been featured on G4 TV, Discovery Channel, Space, IFC, Starz, *Reviews on the Run* and numerous other video media outlets. Rob himself has appeared in the zombie documentary *Zombiemania* (2008) as a zombie authority, sharing time with George A. Romero, Tom Savini, Max Brooks, and other zombie-culture notables. He has also been interviewed for articles appearing in the *Daily Mail*, the *Toronto Star*, the *Huffington Post*, *Wired*, *AOL News* and *Yahoo News*.

Since starting ZombiePortraits.com, Rob Sacchetto has created thousands of zombie portraits, but each and every one is horribly, gruesomely special.

Rob's Zombie Portrait process is dead simple. You choose a portrait type, pay using PayPal and then submit your photo.

Website: www.zombieportraits.com

SPOOKY SUDBURY

Sudbury Tourism

A service website managed by the City of Greater Sudbury, Sudbury Tourism is here to help! Whether it's providing information about Sudbury area vacation packages, uncovering a unique story for media coverage, preparing convention or meeting bids, or simply answering a few questions about visiting Greater Sudbury, you can count on this fantastic website and the staff who manage it for assistance.

Website: www.sudburytourism.ca

Ufology Research

Chris A. Rutkowski is a science writer who has devoted a significant amount of time to investigating and studying reports of UFOs, writing about case investigations, and offering his insights into the broad UFO phenomenon. Two of his previous books published by Dundurn, *Abductions and Aliens* and *The Canadian UFO Report*, were national bestsellers. Rutkowski, who lives just outside Winnipeg, regularly shares updates and reports on this particular blog, which is a fascinating place to get up to date UFO info that is Canadian in origin.

Website: http://uforum.blogspot.ca

Photographer Websites

The following photographers were instrumental in supporting Mark and Jenny in the creation of this book and accompanying materials, and all have either professional photographs or services available. We highly recommend them as being worth checking out.

Greg Roberts — Photographer
www. gregrob.com

RESOURCES

Roger Czerneda — Photographer
www.czernedaphotography.com

John Robbie — Joro Photography
http://jorophotography.com

PUBLICATIONS AND BOOKS

The publications and books listed below are sometimes generic sources, such as the newspapers mentioned, memoirs, or historical accounts of the Sudbury area, or books that bisect some of the subject matter covered in the book — books that might include a reference to Sudbury and area, but which also explore a particular topic or paranormal subject in a broader scope, such as the entire province of Ontario or even Canada. But to us, these are texts worth note for any intrepid readers who are curious to continue to explore more of the same type of reading that captured and intrigued them while enjoying *Spooky Sudbury*.

Northern Life

Northern Life is a twice-weekly (Tuesdays and Thursdays) community newspaper produced by Laurentian Media Group, who also produces such publications as *Northern Ontario Business*, *Sudbury Mining Solutions Journal* and *Sudbury Living*.
    Website: www.northernlife.ca

Sudbury Star

Published in Sudbury by Sun Media, the *Sudbury Star* is the largest circulation daily newspaper in northeastern Ontario.

SPOOKY SUDBURY

Over the years, the paper has been owned by Thomson Newspapers (1950) and Osprey Media (2001) before Sun Media took over the operation in 2007, but has long valued the tradition of delivering the latest news, events and information for the Sudbury community, with an editorial staff and direction deeply rooted in the city's history and committed to being an active and engaged participant in Sudbury's future.

Website: www.thesudburystar.com

Street Names of Downtown Sudbury
(L. Bonin and G. Hallsworth, 1997)

Published by Sudbury's Scrivener Press, this historical directory contains entries on 454 recent and former street names, along with black and white period photographs, pen and ink illustrations, as well as maps that chart the growth and evolution of Sudbury's downtown.

Book page, publisher's website: www.scrivenerpress.com/default.asp?id=571

Hidden Ontario: Secrets from Ontario's Past
(Terry Boyle, 2011)

From the publisher:

"Terry Boyle unveils the eccentric and bizarre in these mini-histories of Ontario's towns and cities: the imposter who ran the Rockwood Asylum in Kingston; Ian Fleming's inspiration for James Bond; the Prince of Wales's undignified crossing of Rice Lake; the tragic life of Joseph Brant; the man who advertised his wife's death before poisoning her; as well as Ontario's first bullfight and the answer to the question, 'Why did so many lumberjacks sport beards?'

The colourful characters, Native legends, and incredible tales

242

RESOURCES

that make up our province's fascinating past come alive in *Hidden Ontario*. From Bancroft, Baldoon, and Brighton to Timmins, Toronto, and Trenton, find out more about the Ontario you thought you knew.

Terry Boyle, who currently lives near Burk's Falls, Ontario, is an author, lecturer, and teacher who has shared his passion for history and folklore in many books since 1976, including four titles on haunted Ontario. He has hosted television's *Creepy Canada* and radio's *Discover Ontario* on Classical 103.1 FM. Boyle lectures and leads haunted tour walks for pleasure."

Author's website: www.entwoodcottage.ca/index.htm

Haunted Ontario: Ghostly Inns, Hotels, and Other Eerie Places (Terry Boyle, 2013)

From the publisher:

"Just when you thought it was safe to turn off the lights, ghost hunter Terry Boyle returns with a revised version of his bestselling Haunted Ontario. Join Terry as he conjures up a treasury of spectral delights that include apparitions at the former Swastika Hotel in Muskoka, the woman in the window at Inn at the Falls in Bracebridge, and poltergeists galore in Toronto's Royal Ontario Museum.

Venture — if you dare — on a ghost hunt to inns, hotels, and museums. Travel with your mind, and perhaps your body, too, to restaurants and private homes. Experience rattling doorknobs, slamming doors, faces in mirrors, and flickering lights. Read accounts from former skeptics and feel their nervous tension as they relate experiences of shadowy visitors, ghostly voices, and household objects that mysteriously disappear. Watch a television show when the set is unplugged and hear tales of vanishing sailors - boats and all.

SPOOKY SUDBURY

With a list of addresses, phone numbers, and websites to each location, Terry Boyle invites all ghost enthusiasts along for the adventure. Feeling brave? You might just want to stop and visit some ghosts on your next trip."

Author's website: www.entwoodcottage.ca/index.htm

Ontario's Ghost Town Heritage (Ron Brown, 2007)

From the publisher:

"As international travel becomes more difficult, there is a renewed interest in exploring our own backyard. Ontario historian Ron Brown visits vestiges of once-thriving towns and villages. Some still maintain small resident populations, while others exist only as abandoned buildings and foundation ruins. All have in common that they are "ghosts" of their former greatness and that their images evoke their lost legacies. *Ontario's Ghost Town Heritage* features interesting and "ghostly" destinations described in a historical context along with accompanying images, including eighty accessible locations throughout Ontario for the curious to explore."

Author's website: www.ronbrown.ca

Top 115 Unusual Things to See in Ontario (Ron Brown, 2013)

From the publisher:

"Ontario is full of hidden treasures. Down village streets, in city lanes, and along quiet country roads lie the province's most unusual sites — a river that disappears, log cabins in the centre of a major city, even a high-rise privy. All await the curious explorer. In his relentless quest to discover the unusual, Ron Brown has travelled nearly every road in Ontario. This book features 115 of his very best trips.

Thoroughly researched and written in an inviting style, each

RESOURCES

description offers a fascinating story with background, location and accompanying color photograph. Most places are easy to reach from Ontario's major population centers, but there are a few for more adventurous explorers. Among the all-new locations featured in this edition are: Peterborough's canoe museum, Ontario's longest small-town train station, a ghost town worth visiting, the Mimico Asylum, with its new lease on life and the Little Current railway swing bridge."

Author's website: www.ronbrown.ca

Come on Over! Northeastern Ontario A to Z
(Dieter K. Buse and Graeme S. Mount, 2011)

A unique, single-volume historical and cultural compendium which will interest residents and visitors alike.

From the publisher:

"Northeastern Ontario is central to the Canadian experience. It is a region rich in historical firsts, in quickly made and lost fortunes, and in communities that have remade themselves. Elliot Lake morphed from a uranium producing community to a retirement haven, Sudbury from the world's nickel capital into an educational, health, and business centre. The book captures both the allure and the survivor tenacity of the northeast's single-industry towns that either are breaking out of, or are still caught in, the boom and bust cycles punctuating the resource industries Canada's wealth relies on."

Book page, publisher's website: www.scrivenerpress.com/default.asp?id=2249

SPOOKY SUDBURY

Eden's Eyes (Sean Costello, 1989), The Cartoonist (2000), Sandman (2000), Finders Keepers (2002), Here After (2008), Captain Quad (2011)

From author's website:

"Sean Costello was born in Ottawa in 1951 and moved to Sudbury thirty years later with the intention of spending a year practicing anaesthesia and returning to his hometown. Something about the city of Sudbury captivated him. No, it wasn't some indeterminable supernatural pull from the very sacred ground of the city, but something more powerful — it was a cute girl whom he married and settled down with in Sudbury.

From Costello's first novel *Eden's Eyes*, which features a drunken brawl at a popular Sudbury watering hole, to *Captain Quad* which makes full horrific use of the dangers of the trains dumping slag on the city, through to *Finders Keepers* whose twisted dark-humour tale begins in Sudbury and begins to unravel after a freak winter accident on Highway 69, Costello's novels beautifully capture the Sudbury region in the same manner that Stephen King's capture the essence of New England."

Author's website: www.seancostello.net

A Brief History of Old Levack — Michael Kavluk (2005)

This book, which exists as a PDF, was first assembled as "Levack: The Early Years", more or less as it now appears and which began in 1978 when Levack Mayor Jim Coady and other Levack residents were encouraging a local town history book to be created.

Book website: www.oxfordrealestate.com/levack.htm

RESOURCES

Haunted Hamilton: The Ghosts of Dundurn Castle and Other Steeltown Shivers (Mark Leslie, 2012)

From the publisher:

"From the Hermitage ruins to Dundurn Castle, from the Customs House to Stoney Creek Battlefield Park, the city of Hamilton, Ontario, is steeped in a rich history and culture. But beneath the surface of the Steel City there dwells a darker heart — from the shadows of yesteryear arise the unexplainable, the bizarre, and the chilling. This collection of tales compiled from historical documents, first-person accounts, and the files of the paranormal group Haunted Hamilton."

Author's website: www.markleslie.ca

Spring Fever (Melanie Marttila, 1997), Neoverse (1998)

At the age of seven, Melanie submitted her first story to CBC's "Pencil Box." Since that first taste of releasing her creative talent into the world, she has become a published poet and an award-winning short story writer. A member of the Sudbury Writers' Guild, an associate member of the League of Canadian Poets, and a professional member of the Canadian Authors Association, in 1999, Mel received her MA in English Literature and Creative Writing from the University of Windsor. Melanie spends her days as a corporate trainer, course designer and training coordinator and by night, as she likes to joke, she braves the tyranny of the empty page, continually working on new short writing and a novel. She maintains that she will continue to write until age and infirmity deprive her of the ability.

Author's website: www. melaniemarttila.ca

SPOOKY SUDBURY

Temperance Lloyd: Hanged for Witchcraft 1682
(B. Chris Nash, 2012)

From the publisher:

"Temperance Lloyd, Susannah Edwards and Mary Trembles of Bideford were the last three women hanged in England as witches, in 1682. Why?

Educated, thinking people sent them to the gallows. The man we know for the King James Bible legalized the hunting and killing of hundreds of his own subjects. Physicians, trained only in "Discourse", accused the natural healers of witchcraft. The women were declared guilty because, according to the Church, to deny witchcraft was to deny God; convicted on hearsay evidence; and executed to appease an angry mob. But who were they? This novel invites you between the lines of history to witness their lives and deaths.

This historical novel questions accepted notions of Time. Perhaps Temperance is still with today's herbalists. What if those old men in the dark corner of every bar have been there forever? Are there still leaders living in the paranoid shadows of a personal trauma?

Come meet Temperance, Susannah, and Mary. Then please remember them, "In the Hope of an End to Persecution and Intolerance", by signing a Petition to the UK, Government to Pardon of Temperance Lloyd, Susannah Edwards and Mary Trembles for the crimes they could not have committed."

Book page, publisher's website: www.friesenpress.com/bookstore/title/119734000007801761

The Canadian UFO Report: The Best Cases Revealed
(Chris Rutkowski and Geoff Dittman, 2006)

From the publisher:

248

RESOURCES

"*The Canadian UFO Report* is a popular history of the UFO phenomenon in Canada, something that has captured the imaginations of young and old alike. Drawn from government documents and civilian case files - many previously unpublished - the book includes a chronological overview of the best Canadian UFO cases, from the very first sighting of 'fiery serpents' over Montreal in 1662 to reports from the past year. There are chapters on the government's involvement with UFOs, UFO landing pads, media interest, and even UFO abductions.

What were the 'ghost airplanes' seen over the Parliament Buildings in 1915, or the flying saucers seen by military officers over Goose Bay Air Force Base, Newfoundland, in the 1940s and 1950s? Was a prospector burned by a UFO in Manitoba in 1967? Did a UFO crash off the coast of Nova Scotia? Was Quebec invaded by UFOs in 1973? Find out here."

Rutkowski's page, publisher's website: www.dundurn.com/authors/chris_rutkowski

Dittman's page, publisher's website: www.dundurn.com/authors/geoff_dittman

Between a Rock and a Hard Place: A Historical Geography of the Finns in the Sudbury Area (Oiva W. Saarinen, 1999)

From the publisher:

"Where else can that well-known phrase be better applied than to a study of the Finns in Sudbury? "Rock" defines the physical reality of the Sudbury setting: rugged hills, mines, farms and forests set in the Precambrian Shield. "Hard" defines the human setting: Finnish immigrants having to contend with the problems and stresses of relocating to a new culture, with livelihoods that required great endurance as well as a tolerance for hazardous conditions.

Since 1883, Finnish immigrants in Sudbury, men and women alike, have striven to improve their lot through the options available to them. Despite great obstacles, the Finns never flagged in their unwavering fight for workers' rights and the union movement. And as agricultural settlers, labour reformers, builders of churches, halls, saunas and athletic fields, Finns left an indelible imprint on the physical and human land-scape. In the process they have played an integral part in the transformation of Sudbury from a small struggling rail town to its present role as regional capital of northwestern Ontario.

This penetrating study of the cultural geography of the Finns in the Sudbury region provides an international, national and local framework for analysis — a model for future studies of other cultural groups."

Book page, publisher's website: www.wlupress.wlu.ca/Catalog/saarinen.shtml

From Meteorite Impact to Constellation City: A Historical Geography of Greater Sudbury (Oiva A. Saarinen, 2013)

From the publisher:

"*From Meteorite Impact to Constellation City* is a historical geography of the City of Greater Sudbury. The story that began billions of years ago encompasses dramatic physical and human events. Among them are volcanic eruptions, two meteorite impacts, the ebb and flow of continental glaciers, Aboriginal occupancy, exploration and mapping by Europeans, exploitation by fur traders and Canadian lumbermen and American entrepreneurs, the rise of global mining giants, unionism, pollution and re-greening, and the creation of a unique constellation city of 160,000.

The title posits the book's two main themes, one physical in nature and the other human: the great meteorite impact of some

RESOURCES

1.85 billion years ago and the development of Sudbury from its inception in 1883. Unlike other large centres in Canada that exhibit a metropolitan form of development with a core and surrounding suburbs, Sudbury developed in a pattern resembling a cluster of stars of differing sizes.

Many of Sudbury's most characteristic attributes are undergoing transformation. Its rocky terrain and the negative impact from mining companies are giving way to attractive neighbourhoods and the planting of millions of trees. Greater Sudbury's blue-collar image as a union powerhouse in a one-industry town is also changing; recent advances in the fields of health, education, retailing, and the local and international mining supply and services sector have greatly diversified its employment base. This book shows how Sudbury evolved from a village to become the regional centre for northeastern Ontario and a global model for economic diversification and environmental rehabilitation."

Book page, publisher's website: www.wlupress.wlu.ca/Catalog/saarinen-meteorite.shtml

The Neanderthal Parallax: (Robert J. Sawyer) Hominids (2002), Humans (2003), Hybrids (2003)

From the publisher:

"This trilogy examines two unique species that are alien to each other, yet bound together by the never-ending quest for knowledge and, beneath their differences, a common humanity. We are one of those species, the other is the Neanderthals of a parallel world where they, not Homo sapiens, became the dominant intelligence. In that world, Neanderthal civilization has reached heights of culture and science comparable to our own, but is very different in history, society, and philosophy.

During a risky experiment deep in a mine in Canada, Ponter

Boddit, a Neanderthal physicist, accidentally pierces the barrier between worlds and is transferred to our universe, where in the same mine (the Neutrino Observatory at Creighton Mine) another experiment is taking place. Hurt, but alive, he is almost immediately recognized as a Neanderthal, but only much later as a scientist. He is captured and studied, alone and bewildered, a stranger in a strange land. But Ponter is also befriended-by a doctor and a physicist who share his questing intelligence and boundless enthusiasm for the world's strangeness, and especially by Laurentian University geneticist Mary Vaughan, a lonely woman with whom he develops a special rapport.

Contact between humans and Neanderthals creates a relationship fraught with conflict, philosophical challenge, and threat to the existence of one species or the other-or both-but equally rich in boundless possibilities for cooperation and growth on many levels, from the practical to the esthetic to the scientific to the spiritual."

Author's website: www.sfwriter.com

Bluffs: Northeastern Ontario Stories from the Edge (Edited by Laurence Steven, 2006)

From the publisher:

"After reading the twenty stories Your Scrivener Press published in *Outcrops: Northeastern Ontario Short Stories* (October 2005), you might feel you know the lay of the region's fictional landscape. Well get ready to have your horizon expanded!

Bluffs presents a wonder-working miscellany of nineteen stories, again by acclaimed, established, and emerging authors.

The collection is a sampler of forms, styles, and genres. Knowing how to "call" these Bluffs isn't easy. Though they present characteristics of ghost stories, science fiction, mystery, satire, folktale, dark comedy, magic realism, meta-fiction, what's

RESOURCES

common among the stories is how they surprise our expectations. Their world is not our world, though it may look like it initially. If we follow their lead, they take us to the various edges of what we know. From their cliff-edges we can both look back at our no-longer-familiar landscape and step forward into your literary landscape … or step into theirs."

Book page, publisher's website: www.scrivenerpress.com/default.asp?id=796

Mysterious Ontario: Myths, Murders, Mysteries and Legends (Geordie Telfer, 2011)

From the publisher:

"Ontario's history is brimming with unexplained events that have confounded residents from the dawn of prehistory to the present. Unlock the past, and discover Ontario's secrets, unsolved disappearances, ghostly encounters and more."

Book page, publisher's website: www.lonepinepublishing.com/cat/9781926695174

Sudbury: Rail Town to Regional Capital (C.M. Wallace and Ashley Thomson, 1996)

From the publisher:

"At the turn of the century Sudbury was a town set on the railway line, with a population of about 2,000. The community was smaller than Sault Ste. Marie and Copper Cliff to the west, and to the east, North Bay and Pembroke. Now, nearly one hundred years later, Sudbury is the largest city in northeastern Ontario. it is also the centre of many governmental, business, social, educational, media, medical, and other professional services in the region.

Sudbury: Rail Town to Regional Capital, which honours the centenary of the community's incorporation as a town in 1893,

SPOOKY SUDBURY

analyses Sudbury decade by decade, describing the ongoing changes in the community and their impact on citizens. The book also examines the forces that shaped the city's destiny and argues that Sudbury is far more than a single-industry town based on mining. Grounded in new research and written in an accessible style by a team of local scholars, the book, with numerous maps and photographs will appeal to urban historians as well as the general reader both within and beyond the city."

Wallace's page, publisher's website: www.dundurn.com/authors/cm_wallace

Thomson's page, publisher's website: www.dundurn.com/authors/ashley_thomson

Notes

Preface and Introduction

1. Mark Leslie, "From Out of the Night," *One Hand Screaming* (Hamilton: Stark Publishing, 2004), 25.
2. *Ibid.* 30.
3. Jenny Jelen, "The True Story of How I Became an Author," *Northern Life*, April 3, 2013.
4. Mark Leslie, "Erratic Cycles," *One Hand Screaming* (Hamilton: Stark Publishing, 2004), 58.
5. Wikipedia, "Fear Series," http://en.wikipedia.org/wiki/Fear_series.

Sudbury Spooks

1. Kennedy Gordon, "Author in search of Spooky," *Sudbury Star*, October 25, 1999.
2. Stanley Coren, *Sleep Thieves: An Eye-opening Exploration into the Science & Mysteries of Sleep* (New York: The Free Press, 1996), 48.
3. *Ibid.,* 49.
4. *Ibid.* 50.
5. *Ibid.* 209.
6. Angie Gallop, "Man for all Seasons," *Sault Star*, June 12, 2010.
7. *Ibid.*
8. *Ibid.*

SPOOKY SUDBURY

9.   *Ibid.*
10. Charlie Smith, *The Beast that God has Kissed: Songs from Birch Lake Road*, (Sudbury: Scrivener Press, 2001).

SCARY SUDBURY SKIES

1.   Reuben Stone, *Encyclopedia of the Unexplained* (Leicester: Bookmart Ltd, 1993), 7.
2.   Una McGovern, Chambers Dictionary of the Unexplained (Edinburgh: Chambers Harrap Publishers Ltd, 2007), 698.
3.   Reuben Stone, *Encyclopedia of the Unexplained* (Leicester: Bookmart Ltd, 1993), 5.
4.   *Ibid.* 5.
5.   *Ibid.* 5–6.
6.   *Ibid.* 6.
7.   Una McGovern, Chambers Dictionary of the Unexplained, (Edinburgh: Chambers Harrap Publishers Ltd, 2007), 698–699.
8.   *Ibid.* 699.
9.   *Ibid.* 699.
10. Michael Whitehorse, "The S Files: Sudbury popular with intergalactic visitors," *Northern Life*, August 6, 1999.
11. "Flying Saucers in Debut Here," *Sudbury Star*, September 23, 1947.
12. "Rocket Seen Leaving Trail," *Sudbury Star*, December 13, 1947.
13. "Mysterious Flame in Sky Nearly Hit Him, Says Driver." *Sudbury Star*, March 20, 1948.
14. James Schefter, *The Race: The Complete True Story of How America Beat Russian to the Moon* (New York: Knopf Doubleday Publishing Group, 2000), 5.
15. C. M. Wallace & Ashley Thomson, *Sudbury: Rail Town to Regional Capital* (Toronto: Dundurn Press Limited, 1993), 191.
16. *Ibid.* 200.
17. "Saw Flash, Flying Fragments in Sky, Says Cartier Railroader," *Sudbury Daily Star*, February 4, 1950.
18. "'Round, Silvery White Object Reported in Sky at Whitefish," *Sudbury Daily Star*, March 21, 1950.
19. "'Silver-Shaped Disc Affair' Spotted in Sky," *Sudbury Daily Star*, May 8, 1950.
20. "'Huge, 100-MPH Hawk' Spotted by City Strollers Thursday," *Sudbury Daily Star*, May 26, 1950.
21. "'Saucers' Seen in Garson Area," *Sudbury Daily Star*, August 8, 1950.

Endnotes

22. "Sudburian Races Flying Saucer Along Highway from Turbine," *Sudbury Daily Star*, November 6, 1951.
23. *Ibid.*
24. "Flying Saucers or Bingo Cards — Who Knows?" *Sudbury Daily Star*, November 8, 1952.
25. "'Flying Saucers' Back Again As Lad Spots Red-White Light," *Sudbury Daily Star*, November 15, 1952.
26. "2 'Flying Torpedoes" Observed For ½ Hour Over Copper Cliff," *Sudbury Daily Star*, January 31, 1953
27. "Flying Objects in the Sky Reported at Several Points, Mostly 'Headed to Lake,'" *Sudbury Daily Star*, February 2, 1953.
28. "Jet Was Over City Thursday; 'Saucers' Still Reported," *Sudbury Daily Star*, February 3, 1953.
29. *Ibid.*
30. "'Saucer' Seen Near Sudbury Third Time in Two Weeks," *Sudbury Daily Star*, February 14, 1953.
31. "'Crescent Shape in Blue Mist' Latest in the Sky," *Sudbury Daily Star*, February 16, 1953.
32. "Red Ball Joins Saucer Host in Skies Over Sudbury Area," *Sudbury Daily Star*, February 17, 1953.
33. *Ibid.*
34. "There's Still Something in the Sky!" *Sudbury Daily Star*, February 24, 1953.
35. *Ibid.*
36. "That 'Thing' Is Back Again in Sudbury Sky," *Sudbury Daily Star*, April 14, 1953.
37. *Ibid.*
38. "That 'Thing' Back Over City, Seen by Burton Ave Residents," *Sudbury Daily Star*, August 8, 1953.
39. "Martin Visitors at Garson Police Scoff Women Scared," *Sudbury Daily Star*, July 6, 1954.
40. *Ibid.*
41. "'Saucer People' Keep Eye on Sudbury District," *Sudbury Daily Star*, July 13, 1954.
42. "Martin Visitors at Garson Police Scoff Women Scared," *Sudbury Daily Star*, July 6, 1954.
43. "'Saucer People' Keep Eye on Sudbury District," *Sudbury Daily Star*, July 13, 1954.
44. *Ibid.*
45. "Glowing Ball Reported Seen In Bay Sky," *Sudbury Daily Star*, September 1, 1954.

46. "Report 'Flying Saucer' From Timmins District," *Sudbury Daily Star*, September 2, 1954.

47. "Flying Object Back In Sky Over North Bay," *Sudbury Daily Star*, September 7, 1954.

48. "Saucer Now Triangular, Seen by Two Sudburians," *Sudbury Daily Star*, September 21, 1954.

49. "Kirkland Bush Pilot Admits Taking Up 'Flying Saucer,'" *Sudbury Daily Star*, January 13, 1955.

50. "'Flying Saucer' Seen at Sturgeon," *Sudbury Daily Star*, August 3, 1955.

51. "Those Flying Saucers Are Back Again," *Sudbury Daily Star*, March 21, 1956.

52. "Whitish Light in Sky May Have Been a Comet," *Sudbury Daily Star*, August 12, 1957.

53. "City Boy, 15, Follows Track of White Light," *Sudbury Daily Star*, August 1957.

54. "Suspect Fireball Over City May Be Meteor Passing By," *Sudbury Daily Star*, August 27, 1957.

55. "'Bright Light' Could Be Planet Venus," *Sudbury Daily Star*, December 3, 1957.

56. C. M. Wallace & Ashley Thomson, *Sudbury: Rail Town to Regional Capital* (Toronto: Dundurn Press Limited, 1993), 199.

57. "Levack Astronomer Saw 'Fireball' Over District," *Sudbury Daily Star*, July 19, 1958.

58. C. M. Wallace & Ashley Thomson, *Sudbury: Rail Town to Regional Capital* (Toronto: Dundurn Press Limited, 1993), 190–192.

59. C. M. Wallace & Ashley Thomson, *Sudbury: Rail Town to Regional Capital* (Toronto: Dundurn Press Limited, 1993), 219.

60. "Sudbury in the 1960s," *Sudbury Star*, October 29, 2008.

61. "Flying Saucers? High School Girls See Strange Object," *Sudbury Daily Star*, July 13, 1960.

62. "Flying Object Like 'Beach Ball,'" *Sudbury Daily Star*, November 7, 1960.

63. "'Flying Saucer' Chases City Motorist, He Stopped, Took Look, Got Scared," *Sudbury Daily Star*, February 10, 1961.

64. "'Visitors from Outer Space' Liked What They Saw … Back Second Night in Row," *Sudbury Daily Star*, February 11, 1961.

65. "Report New Sighting of Red Flying Object," *Sudbury Daily Star*, February 14, 1961.

66. "See Large Objects in Creighton Sky," *Sudbury Daily Star*, September 15, 1961.

67. "Three Area Men Sight Object, Identity Unknown," *Sudbury Daily Star*,

ENDNOTES

January 28, 1966.

68. "Elliot Lake Youths Spot Flying Object Heading Northeast," *Sudbury Daily Star*, March 31, 1966.

69. "Flying Object Reported Tuesday," *Sudbury Daily Star*, July 19, 1967.

70. "Teenager Says Flying Object Tried to Land," *Sudbury Daily Star*, October 11, 1967.

71. "UFO Seen Over City; Eighth in Two Months Reported in District," *Sudbury Daily Star*, November 8, 1967.

72. "Reports Seeing Flying Object on Weekend," *Sudbury Daily Star*, December 4, 1967.

73. "Some People Laugh, Just Won't Believe," *Sudbury Daily Star*, November 22, 1967.

74. "Laurentian Students Claim They Photographed 'Saucer,'" *Sudbury Daily Star*, January 24, 1968.

75. *Ibid.*

76. *Ibid.*

77. *Ibid.*

78. "Teen-agers See Flying Object," *Sudbury Daily Star*, August 15, 1968.

79. "Elliot Lake Man Sights a UFO; 'Like a Star,'" *Sudbury Daily Star*, November 26, 1968.

80. "Walford Area Men See 'Red Fire Ball,'" *Sudbury Daily Star*, July 28, 1969.

81. C. M. Wallace & Ashley Thomson, *Sudbury: Rail Town to Regional Capital* (Toronto: Dundurn Press Limited, 1993), 242–243.

82. C. M. Wallace & Ashley Thomson, *Sudbury: Rail Town to Regional Capital* (Toronto: Dundurn Press Limited, 1993), 244.

83. C. M. Wallace & Ashley Thomson, *Sudbury: Rail Town to Regional Capital* (Toronto: Dundurn Press Limited, 1993), 246.

84. "See Silver Object In Northern Sky, Disappeared Fast," *Sudbury Daily Star*, November 4, 1970.

85. "Pilot Reports Sighting UFO at Whitefish," *Sudbury Daily Star*, March 7, 1972.

86. "UFO Sightings Reported in Hanmer and Sudbury," *Sudbury Daily Star*, July 28, 1972.

87. "Lake Ramsey UFO sighted at hospital," *Sudbury Star*, August 15, 1975.

88. "Manitoulin boy claims sighting flashing UFO past five nights," *Sudbury Star*, August 7, 1975.

89. "UFO reported seen on Island on five of six nights in row, but fails to show for reporter," *Sudbury Star*, August 9, 1975.

90. *Ibid.*

SPOOKY SUDBURY

91. *Ibid.*
92. "Shining UFO sighted by nine on Manitoulin," *Sudbury Star*, August 12, 1975.
93. "Manitoulin UFO sighted tenth time," *Sudbury Star*, August 16, 1975.
94. "Radar base, police see UFO here," *Sudbury Star*, November 11, 1975.
95. *Ibid.*
96. *Ibid.*
97. *Ibid.*
98. "US jets scrambled on UFOs," *Sudbury Star*, November 12, 1975.
99. UFO Casebook, "UFOs Intrude into SAC Base Weapons Area: October-November 1975," http://www.ufocasebook.com/sacbaseweapons1975.html.
100. *Ibid.*
101. *Ibid.*
102. Chris A. Rutkowski and Geoff Dittman, *The Canadian UFO Report: The Best Cases Revealed* (Toronto: Dundurn Press Limited, 2006), 114.
103. "US jets scrambled on UFOs," *Sudbury Star*, November 12, 1975.
104. Chris A. Rutkowski and Geoff Dittman, *The Canadian UFO Report: The Best Cases Revealed* (Toronto: Dundurn Press Limited, 2006), 115–116.
105. C. M. Wallace and Ashley Thomson, *Sudbury: Rail Town to Regional Capital* (Toronto: Dundurn Press Limited, 1993), 275.
106. C. M. Wallace and Ashley Thomson, *Sudbury: Rail Town to Regional Capital* (Toronto: Dundurn Press Limited, 1993), 276–277.
107. C. M. Wallace and Ashley Thomson, *Sudbury: Rail Town to Regional Capital* (Toronto: Dundurn Press Limited, 1993), 280.
108. Science North, "History," http://www.sciencenorth.ca/about/our-organization/index.aspx?id=821.
109. Science North, "Our Mission," http://www.sciencenorth.ca/.
110. Ken Wallenius, "UFOlogist changing attitudes," *Sudbury Star*, May 4, 1991.
111. Michel Deschamps, NOUFORS, "2013 Sighting Reports," http://www.noufors.com/2013_sighting_reports.html.
112. CBC.ca, "Canadian government no longer investigating UFOs," http://www.cbc.ca/news/canada/nova-scotia/story/2013/03/07/ns-ufo-investigation.html.

SPECULATIVE SUDBURY

1. Ontario Sasquatch, "Aboriginal Names for Sasquatch," http://www.ontariosasquatch.com/#/aboriginal-names/4522705733.

Endnotes

2. *Ibid.*
3. Wikipedia, "Patterson-Gimlin film," http://en.wikipedia.org/wiki/Patterson-Gimlin_film.
4. Ontario Bigfoot, "Sightings," http://www.ontariobigfoot.com/Sightings.html.
5. *Ibid.*
6. *Ibid.*
7. *Ibid.*
8. Ontario Sasquatch, "Report Database," http://www.ontariosasquatch.com/#/report-database/4520961175.
9. Bigfoot Research Organization, "Report #18375 (Class B)," http://www.bfro.net/GDB/show_report.asp?id=18375.
10. Ontario Sasquatch, "Report Database," http://www.ontariosasquatch.com/#/nipissing/4521082945.
11. Ontario Sasquatch, "Report Database," http://www.ontariosasquatch.com/#/timiskaming/4521082964.
12. "Strange creature found in northern Ontario," *Sudbury Star*, May 21, 2010.
13. *Ibid.*
14. *Ibid.*
15. Wikipedia, "Ogopogo," http://en.wikipedia.org/wiki/Ogopogo.
16. Wikipedia, "Memphre," http://en.wikipedia.org/wiki/Memphre.
17. Wikipedia, "Igopogo," http://en.wikipedia.org/wiki/Igopogo.
18. Wikipedia, "Mussie," http://en.wikipedia.org/wiki/Mussie.

Strange Sudbury

1. Wikipedia, "Witchcraft," http://en.wikipedia.org/wiki/Witchcraft
2. Jenny Jelen, "Writing Together: Chris and Roger Nash celebrate joint book launch," *Northern Life*, November 23, 2012.
3. SWNS.com, "Campaign to clear names of three women hanged for witchcraft three centuries ago," http://swns.com/news/campaign-to-clear-names-of-three-women-hanged-for-witchcraft-three-centuries-ago-24072/.
4. *Ibid.*
5. Laura Stradiotto, "Sudbury inspires horror," *Sudbury Star*, July 7, 2012.
6. Wikipedia, "Brigitte Kingsley," http://en.wikipedia.org/wiki/Brigitte_Kingsley
7. Laura Stradiotto, "Sudbury inspires horror," *Sudbury Star*, July 7, 2012.
8. *Ibid.*

SPOOKY SUDBURY

9.   *Ibid.*
10. *Ibid.*
11. Sudbury Northern Life Staff, "Sudbury's Brigitte Kingsley tackles fourth Summer Vale project," *Northern Life*, July 12, 2012.
12. *Ibid.*
13. *Ibid.*
14. *Ibid.*
15. Ron Brown, *Ontario's Ghost Town Heritage* (Erin: Boston Mills Press, 2007), 7.
16. Wikipedia, "Burwash, Ontario," http://en.wikipedia.org/wiki/Burwash,_Ontario.
17. *Ibid.*
18. Ron Brown, *Ontario's Ghost Town Heritage* (Erin: Boston Mills Press, 2007), 19.
19. Ron Brown, *Ontario's Ghost Town Heritage* (Erin: Boston Mills Press, 2007), 182.
20. *Ibid.*
21. *Ibid.*
22. Ontario Ghost Towns, "Benny," http://www.ghosttownpix.com/ontario/intros/benn.html.
23. Ron Brown, *Ontario's Ghost Town Heritage* (Erin: Boston Mills Press, 2007), 135.
24. *Ibid.*
25. *Ibid.*
26. *Ibid.*
27. Ontario Ghost Towns, "Benny," http://www.ghosttownpix.com/ontario/intros/benn.html.
28. Wikipedia, "Biscotasing, Ontario," http://en.wikipedia.org/wiki/Biscotasing,_Ontario.
29. Ron Brown, *Ontario's Ghost Town Heritage* (Erin: Boston Mills Press, 2007), 138.
30. *Ibid.*
31. Wikipedia, "Grey Owl," http://en.wikipedia.org/wiki/Grey_Owl.
32. *Ibid.*
33. Ron Brown, *Ontario's Ghost Town Heritage* (Erin: Boston Mills Press, 2007), 138.
34. *Ibid.*
35. Michael Barnes, *Great Northern Ontario Mines* (Burnstown: General Store Publishing House, 1998), 44.
36. *Ibid.* 44.

ENDNOTES

37. *Ibid.*46
38. SNOLAB, "About SNOLAB," http://www.snolab.ca/about.
39. *Ibid.*
40. Michael Barnes, *Great Northern Ontario Mines* (Burnstown: General Store Publishing House, 1998), 46.
41. SNOLAB, "SNOLAB Underground Facilities", http://www.snolab.ca/facility/underground.
43. Michael Barnes, *Great Northern Ontario Mines* (Burnstown: General Store Publishing House, 1998), 49.
43. SNOLAB, "Science at SNOLAB," http://www.snolab.ca/science.
44. *Ibid.*
45. Laura Stradiotto, "Sudbury inspires horror," *Sudbury Star*, July 7, 2012.
46. *Ibid.*
47. *Ibid.*
48. *Ibid.*
49. *Ibid.*
50. *Ibid.*
51. Jenny Jelen, "On the set with Peter Mihaichuk," *Northern Life*, May 20, 2011.
52. *Ibid.*
53. *Ibid.*
54. Laura Stradiotto, "Sudbury inspires horror," *Sudbury Star*, July 7, 2012
55. *Ibid.*
56. *Ibid.*
57. Jenny Jelen, "On the set with Peter Mihaichuk," *Northern Life*, May 20, 2011.
58. The Official Donnelly Home Page, "Donnelly Bookshelf," http://www.donnellys.com/Books.html.
59. *Ibid.*
60. Wikipedia, "Thomas P. Kelley," http://en.wikipedia.org/wiki/Thomas_P._Kelley.
61. Orlo Miller, *The Donnellys Must Die* (Missisauga: John Wiley & Sons Canada Ltd., 2007).
62. The Official Donnelly Home Page, "Frequently Asked Questions," http://www.donnellys.com/Questions.htm.
63. *Ibid.*
64. Judy Pearsall and Bill Trumble, *Oxford English Language Dictionary* (Toronto: Oxford University Press, 1996), 52.
65. Una McGovern, *Chambers Dictionary of the Unexplained* (Edinburgh: Chambers Harrap Publishers Ltd, 2007), 268.

SPOOKY SUDBURY

66. *Ibid.* 269.
67. Laurentian University Website, "Behavioural Neuroscience: People," http://oldwebsite.laurentian.ca/neurosci/_people/Persinger.htm.
68. *Ibid.*
69. *Ibid.*
70. Wikipedia, "God Helmet," http://en.wikipedia.org/wiki/God_helmet.
71. Michael Valpy, "Is God all in our heads?" *Globe and Mail* (August 25, 2001), F7.
72. Jack Hitt, "This is Your Brain on God," *Wired*, (November 1999), Issue 7.11
73. *Ibid.*
74. Gordie Telfer, *Mysterious Ontario: Myths, Murders and Legends* (Toronto: Quagmire Press Ltd, 2011), 118
75. "Dr. Persinger's God Helmet," YouTube (accessed February 22, 2013), http://www.youtube.com/watch?v=8YPOTaUyvA0
76. *Ibid.*
77. Gordie Telfer, *Mysterious Ontario: Myths, Murders and Legends* (Toronto: Quagmire Press Ltd, 2011), 117.
78. Susan Blackmore, "Alien Abduction," *New Scientist* (November 19, 1994), 29–31
79. Susan Blackmore, "Abduction by Alien or Sleep Paralysis?" *Skeptical Inquirer* (May/June 1998), vol. 22.3.
80. Una McGovern, Chambers Dictionary of the Unexplained (Edinburgh: Chambers Harrap Publishers Ltd, 2007), 628.
81. David J. Hufford, *The Terror That Comes in the Night* (Philadelphia: University of Pennsylvania Press, 1982), 3.
82. Una McGovern, *Chambers Dictionary of the Unexplained* (Edinburgh: Chambers Harrap Publishers Ltd, 2007), 628.